About the author

Perry Wood studied music at the Guildhall School of Music and worked a a professional musician until 1990, when he moved to Exmoor to work with horses. Gradually his career began to include teaching communication skills to senior executives in major corporations. A ground-breaking workshop leader, musician and published author, today Perry Wood lives in the South West of England.

By the same author:

Real Riding (2002)
Practical Horse Whispering (2003)

SECRETS
OF THE
PEOPLE
WHISPERER

Using the art of communication
to enhance your own life,
and the lives of others

Perry Wood

RIDER

LONDON · SYDNEY · AUCKLAND · JOHANNESBURG

1 3 5 7 9 10 8 6 4 2

First published in 2004 by Rider,
an imprint of Ebury Press, Random House,
20 Vauxhall Bridge Road, London SW1V 2SA

Random House Australia (Pty) Limited
20 Alfred Street, Milsons Point, Sydney,
New South Wales 2061, Australia

Random House New Zealand Limited
18 Poland Road, Glenfield,
Auckland 10, New Zealand

Random House South Africa (Pty) Limited
Endulini, 5A Jubilee Road,
Parktown 2193, South Africa

www.randomhouse.co.uk

The Random House Group Limited Reg. No. 954009

Papers used by Rider are natural, recyclable products
made from wood grown in sustainable forests.

Typeset by SX Composing DTP, Rayleigh, Essex
Printed and bound by Mackays of Chatham plc, Chatham, Kent

A CIP catalogue record for this book
is available from the British Library

ISBN 1-8441-3563-2

Dedicated to my dear Esaya;
you gave me so much:
I had never experienced such freedom and joy
until you came into my life
and shared those gifts with me.
God bless your soul

Contents

Acknowledgements

Heartfelt thanks to my family, friends and all those who have supported me regardless of what is happening.

My thanks and respect to Judith Kendra at Rider for her vision, gentleness and professionalism in publishing this book. Thanks also to Sue Lascelles for being a very understanding, talented and patient editor, and to all at Random House who have contributed in bringing this book to life and out into the world.

Thanks and unconditional love to Tenor for being a loyal companion through thick and thin.

Love and thanks to Monte (and his band of happy followers) for setting a great example in how to be a kind, noble and powerful leader.

Thanks to Andrew McFarlane, Elaine Harrison and all at Leadchange: I could not have wished for better people to work with and have as partners. Thanks also to Andrew for being such a model of integrity, and to Elaine for speaking with such intuitive insight that I have, on occasions, been literally floored. My love and thanks to Margrit Coates for being my guardian angel.

Thanks to all of my coaching clients and students: coaching and learning are two-way streets, which mean you have helped and taught me at least as much as I have taught you.

Thanks to Kate Parkes for coming out with cracking gems of wisdom just when I needed them.

Huge thanks to all the people whom I have found challenging, difficult, scary or downright impossible over the years: you may have contributed more to my writing this book than anyone else!

My appreciation to 'the family' at Mataji Yogananda's centre in Somerset for your work in bringing the gifts of pure meditation and Kriya Yoga to so many people, including myself: it really *is* priceless, thank you.

Finally, thanks to anyone who reads this book and, as a result of using the secrets of the people whisperer in their lives, makes the world a more joyful place for themselves and others to live in.

Introduction

I am in the car with my father. We are on our way to the coast to spend a couple of days together. I sense that he is seriously ill and that he may not last beyond Christmas: it is now the end of October. I am afraid about this, not because we are very close, but because we are not very close. We have not really communicated, except on a superficial level, for years.

I had asked him to come away with me so that we might talk. I wanted to make my peace with him, there were things I felt I needed to know from him before he was gone forever and time was running out. Normally it was my mother who did most of the talking while my father lived almost silently in his own reclusive world: reading a novel, watching TV or listening to music with his head phones on.

For the first couple of hours on the journey I was asking myself whether this was such a good idea. Our conversation was on the usual superficial level and I wondered if we were going to get on to anything meaningful that I wanted to hear from him.

Suddenly the conversation opened up: he began to talk and didn't stop talking for two whole days. He told me stuff I wanted to know, stuff I'd wondered about and stuff that had never even entered my head. He told me the reasons why he hadn't wanted children and the reasons he'd decided to have them anyway. He told me how it was for him as a child and how it was for him when he had small children of his own. He told me how money had been for him. He told me how much he loved my mother. He told me how much he loved my brother and me and how proud he was of us. He talked about sex. He told me what he was afraid of, what his fears were and what hurt him even after many decades had passed. He told me things that I hold in my heart and cannot share with you or anyone else.

By releasing all the things that he had kept locked up for so long, by communicating openly and honestly, I finally understood so much about him, and about myself, too. By what he communicated, he had freed me, and I hope that in some way he had freed himself.

Following the trip away with my father, I began to think about all of the significant relationships in my life, past and present, and the effects that communication had on them. I reflected on what adults had communicated to us as children, about how my parents had communicated with each other, how I had lost close touch with my brother. I reflected on how, despite there being a great deal of love, so much of my marriage had been nine years of anger, frustration, feeling unloved, lonely and misunderstood, and how this had finally led to divorce. How the business I had co-run for twelve years, although successful, had been an uphill struggle because of how my partner and I communicated with each other, our staff, suppliers and clients.

It seemed that I had been brilliant at saying the wrong thing, at hurting people's deepest feelings, at being misunderstood or misinterpreting what someone was telling me without ever intending to do so.

If my mouth was open, I would put my foot in it.

If there was something teeth-jarringly inappropriate to say, I would say it.

If there was a way to appear completely uncaring, I would find it.

The two days with my father were a crystallisation of a mystery, the answers to which I had been searching for fifteen years. What I searched for and began to discover are the 'Secrets of the People Whisperer'. Though I should really say 're-discovered', for although the methods presented in this book may appear to be totally new, they have always been there, despite remaining largely hidden from many of us.

Communication, whether good or bad, is a huge issue in every area of all of our lives: in personal, business, family, friendship and intimate relationships. How wonderful and liberating would it be then, to become a highly skilled communicator? A people whisperer? What would it be like to truly understand other people and to be truly understood, to move effortlessly through life with more ease, love, fun and joy?

Everything that happens communicates something. Everything we think do or say is a communication – which means it gives out a message – and each and every message has an impact on shaping our lives, for better or for worse: even love itself is a form of communication. This raises all kinds of exciting possibilities and questions . . .

◆ How do you communicate with your loved ones?
◆ What are you communicating to the environment?
◆ What kind of communications happen in your workplace or business?
◆ If you have a spiritual guide or God in your life, how do you communicate with them and how do they communicate with you?
◆ Most fundamentally: how do you communicate with yourself?

The answers to these questions are some of the secrets of people whispering; that is, to be aware of what you and other people are communicating on every level, mentally, verbally, physically and spiritually, and to be adept at interacting with kindness, understanding, skill, power and subtlety.

The secrets of people whispering work in every situation in our lives: from intimate relationships with loved ones to work environments, even to situations where we and our enemies meet. Some people have always had a few pieces of the jigsaw, some part of the secrets, but it is only now, in the twenty-first century, 'the Communication Age,' with mobile phones, text messaging, e-mails, the Internet and all manner of communication mediums, that the secrets of people whispering have been drawn together in such a way.

I have been very fortunate in needing to improve my communication skills so badly. I was 'asking' to learn and, as the saying goes, 'When the pupil is ready, the teacher appears'. And my teachers did appear.

My master teachers communicate at a very subtle level. They have refined their skills over the last sixty million years to a very high degree and their very survival depends upon it. They do not use words and do not judge; they are noble, quick-witted and very powerful; they sense true intentions, integrity and have an innate sense of justice. These master teachers are horses. When you get your communication wrong with a person, you may end up having an argument or someone sulking. When you get it wrong with half a ton of hyper-sensitive flight animal, you know about it!

I spent a number of years studying some of the great riding masters. I worked training, breeding and starting (breaking in) young horses and developing ways to communicate with these magnificent creatures. My experiences ultimately led to me writing a groundbreaking book about my approach with horses, in order to share some of the knowledge I had accumulated.

As my life and experience with horses expanded, I spent a great deal of time working at the occluded front – where horses and people meet – teaching people to improve their communication with horses and, as an unintended side-effect, helping people to discover how people communicate with themselves.

My experiences of horse whispering led me to see horses as a mirror: they reflect back very clearly whatever it is that you are communicating to them. I then realised that people are, in fact, exactly the same: they also reflect back to you, although sometimes it is difficult to see this because the use of words, judgements, gossip, acting and preconceived notions often act as a smoke-screen.

The discoveries about communication that were surfacing as a result of my years as a professional horseman took me on to another unintended path: that of running 'breakthrough' workshops with horses, coaching executives from major corporations in their leadership and communication skills. My work had taken me from horse whispering into people whispering, so to speak. Both require a high degree of self and other-awareness, to know exactly what you are communicating, intentionally or not, at all times and to truly listen to what others are communicating.

During my work coaching executives in corporations, as well as private individuals, I have seen more and more how we shape every aspect of our lives by the way we communicate with ourselves and others. These communications are often so automatic or so subtle that we are oblivious to them and really do not know what we are communicating: the secrets of people whispering will bring light into your communications and equip you with the tools to create immediate and profound improvements to every interaction you have.

Secrets of the People Whisperer will show you simple and incredible ways to connect with your true self, other people and the world at large on many different levels. It will show you how to understand and be understood; to truly listen and give space in which people can express themselves without fear or judgement; to ask for what you want and have a far greater chance of getting it. Through its guidance, you will come to know others and yourself better on physical, mental and energy levels; you will begin to go beyond personality and allow the true 'being' within yourself and others to shine through. Ultimately, you will discover how to give every relationship and meeting you ever have the best possible chance of success. You will find out how to ask for what you want – and how to get it – from the Universe itself. (What I mean by 'Universe' in the context of this book is anything and everything other than your body and your conscious thoughts: you may wish to think of it as your Higher Self, your subconscious, the environment, God or whatever else makes sense to you.) I suggest that you read one chapter at a time so that you can inwardly digest the essence of each secret before moving on to the next one.

When you make use of the secrets of people whisperer in your life – at home, at work and at play – it is not a gift from me to you, it is a gift from you to yourself. Out of love and respect for yourself and the people in your life, I urge you to give and receive that gift and enjoy the kind of experiences you deserve.

My sense about my father's illness around Christmas-time had been right. On Boxing Day he suddenly became very ill, doubled up with pain in his stomach. He was rushed to hospital where it was discovered that he was suffering from previously un-diagnosed cancer in his gut, and worse, the cancer had punctured a hole through the lining of the gut and caused peritonitis. He was operated on immediately and miraculously survived. After-wards, the surgeon said that had they not operated on him that day he would have been dead the next.

PART I

Communicating With Yourself

Secret One

Know Who You Really Are

WHO ARE YOU REALLY?

During every single relationship or communication you ever have there is always one regular participant: you. No matter how much time you spend with your family, friends, work colleagues or loved ones, there is one person you will always spend more time with than with any of them: you.

It really isn't easy to know anyone very well, and the scary thing is that the person who is often the hardest to get to know is ourselves. But getting to know ourselves is one of the most important things that we can ever do if we want to communicate with anyone else effectively. So the first question is: how do you find out who you really are?

Let's ask another question: who are you *not*? You're not any one of the other six billion or so humans on the planet . . . That means you are totally unique. Wow! Let's ponder that for a moment: there is no one else amongst an unimaginable six billion people who has your fingerprints, your eyes, your teeth, your body, your personality, your experiences *or* your thoughts. That means you're absolutely incredible. In the vastness of time and space, from the Big Bang onwards into the eternal future, across the infinity of the Universe, no one will ever be you – except *you*. That's big! It makes you special beyond words.

So what would you like to do with your unique and extraordinary life? What would you like to express? Who would you like to touch in some way? Would you like to bring love or hate? Will you create beauty or a mess? What difference do you really want to make? Whatever you decide, it's important to remember that however small your contribution may seem to you, the

Universe will know. It cannot but feel what you have done, are doing and will do while you're here in this life. Your contribution will make a difference: it is impossible for it to do otherwise.

So who exactly are you? Are you your body? Are you your mind? Did you first come into being when you were born or when you were conceived? Did you exist in any form before you were conceived? In order to start opening yourself up to your true self and your incredible potential, think again of all the things you've been told about who you are and about how you came into being . . .

What if your body is just a suit that you are wearing until it wears out? Or a costume you're wearing for a particular role in a play, and when the performance is over you'll take it off again? What if your 'personality' or self-identity is a role you are playing in some kind of cosmic theatrical production? And when this performance is over you will stop pretending to be this 'person' and go back to being your real self instead . . . What if your mind is a computer that was completely empty when you started out, but other people have been filling it with 'stuff' since it was first powered up? So now it's so clogged up with 'spam', old programs and deleted files, you don't know which bits you need and which bits you don't . . . And, then, sometimes it crashes for no reason whatsoever!

In truth, our bodies are amazing machines and much of what we programme into our minds is fabulously useful . . . Have a go at this: watch objectively as your body makes a cup of coffee. Put the kettle on; sense how your mind operates your body almost unconsciously; watch the incredibly complex manoeuvres your hands perform with beautiful precision, accuracy and timing – opening the jar, handling the teaspoon like a surgeon at work; scooping just the right amount of coffee and sugar like a master artist, pouring just the right amount of milk . . . And note how normally when you make coffee you don't even think about what you're doing; you chat, watch TV, read or think about something else, somewhere else in the past or future. Your computer mind runs your body and your body carries out these incredible operations all day, every day! How do you do that? How amazing is that?

If your body is a temporary suit and your mind is a sometimes rebellious computer, what else is there? What other parts of you are there when the body is still and your thoughts stop? Your body has probably changed through the time you've had it (I know mine has!), and your mind is constantly developing and being fed new information, so is there anything about you that is a constant? In addition to your changing body and developing mind, somewhere inside you probably feel like the same person now as you always were, even as a small child.

In case you are wondering what all this has to do with people whispering, let me ask you, at what level do you think that true communication really takes place? The answer is that much of what happens in true people whispering occurs at an almost indefinable level, beyond the body and mind.

'The Real You' Beyond Body and Mind

Many people talk about the Soul, Spirit, Inner Energy field, subconscious or many other terms for that part of us that isn't our body and mind. Some people deny its existence because – they argue – we can't see it, measure it or prove it is there.

There is no doubt that to define our spirit or essence in words, ideas, thoughts or form seems practically impossible, but then of course it would be indefinable: the soul is beyond the body and mind. If the body could touch it or the mind could analyse it, then it would be within their reach and not beyond them. (Remember that no one could see, hear, smell, measure or prove that electricity existed until the 1800s: that didn't mean it wasn't there!)

Looking into your own soul

It is said that the eyes are the 'windows of the soul'. Go really close to the mirror with your face and look deeply into the pupils of your own eyes. How does it make you feel? Awe-struck, afraid, uncomfortable, embarrassed, filled with love, uplifted, nothing whatsoever? Stay there for a while and feel whatever comes up. Do you notice yourself looking at one eye more than the other? Do you feel you have to keep looking away? Do you feel drawn further in?

See how you feel when you are upset with someone or something and then go to the mirror and repeat the same exercise.

See how you feel if you do the same exercise with another person (with their permission): take a non-judgemental and unhurried look into their soul by looking deeply into the pupils of their eyes.

Powerful people whisperers

Sometimes people can really inspire us, not by what their bodies look like (although that can be very interesting!), what they say or how their minds work, but somehow by who they really are. When we meet someone who is genuinely comfortable with themselves, someone who knows who they really are, it touches something deep within us that yearns to be touched – to be let out into the light, to be recognised, to be freed to work the miracles that our inner self is waiting to perform for us, if only we would let it. When I work with people and they have even a momentary glimpse into the cavernous infinity of their true inner self, they are stunned, elated and awe-struck by the realisation of their true potential . . . Yet each and every one of us has this vastness and potential within us.

There is only one thing in the whole universe that stops us from living life as our true selves, and that is ourselves. But why would we want to stop ourselves from being who we really are? Perhaps we do this for the same reasons we choose to make life more difficult than it needs to be: perhaps it is for the learning.

And what could possibly hold us back once we allow ourselves to be our *true* selves? The answer is, probably nothing.

Things to do:

1. Look at your hand for a minute or two. Move the fingers around, pick things up, scratch your nose – be amazed! Advancements in science haven't come anywhere near to doing what you can do so effortlessly with just one hand!
2. Go somewhere like a high street, train station or shopping mall where there are lots of people. Sit down and have a good look at

them for at least five minutes. Marvel at how much variety there is: see how no one looks just like you; see how each person has his or her own unique presence.

3. Reflect on your sense of unchanging identity. Think about your sense of yourself as a child and as you are now. Go through your memories and get in touch with the inner you, the 'you' that has always been there since you were very young and is still there now.

4. Check out your body – what it looks like and what you feel about it. Think about all the things you might use your body for during the course of a normal week: walking, eating, sitting, expressing, opening doors, lifting things, laughing, having sex, writing, blowing your nose, eating, drinking, playing, hugging, smelling, touching, feeling pain, talking and hearing. Watch yourself performing tasks automatically.

5. Marvel at how useful and brilliant your mind is: see how it can plan ahead, remember details, operate your body, analyse situations, sort out problems, create problems (Oh dear!), make decisions, engage in conversations and many more things too numerous to mention.

As we begin to take a closer look at who we really are, we may be tempted to categorise or judge whatever we unearth. So let's go one step further on our journey into people whispering by exploring how we can overcome the ways in which we sometimes close ourselves off from truly communicating by being judgemental about ourselves and others.

JUDGEMENT

We spend so much time judging ourselves and the people around us. Even in little ways that we don't notice, we judge our behaviour, our performance, our experiences, our responses and abilities in everything we do; likewise we judge others in the same way. Being judgemental is a social addiction. Read the papers and you will see judgement, judgement, judgement. Listen to people speak about themselves or others: judgement again. Act like a fly on the wall in practically every workplace, drinking bar or home in the world and we will overhear conversation that is carrying judgement with it. Judgement is often the result of comparing how things actually are to how we think they should be; and making that comparison means we are not accepting reality as it really is. By so doing, we create unhappiness and interfere with the flow of true communication.

Passing judgement over ourselves and others stifles possibilities, creates barriers between people and makes us believe in limitation. Judgement creates a vicious circle: if every time we do something we are judged for it, we will become less willing to take action, take risks, be creative, attempt things or allow things to flow because we think we will be judged again – which we will be, by ourselves if not by others! By constantly going over mistakes and shortcomings, real or imagined, we become crippled and stuck in a life of limitation, which means we begin to act in ways that are not who we really are, in order to minimise how much we are judged. If we are judging and thinking about whether what was just done or said was good or bad, we are missing the present moment, which means we are not giving our attention or best abilities to what is happening *now*! Highly successful people don't hang around beating themselves up for failures or judging themselves; they just get on with it.

Not judging yourself doesn't mean that you are indifferent, that you don't care or that you are being irresponsible . . . It means knowing that you are doing the best you can do in that situation with the skills you have at that time. You can always turn around and say you could have done better or you should have done something different, but at the time you did what you did. That was what you were meant to do at the time. Accept it and move forwards.

Transcend judgement by accepting yourself, other people and things just the way they are, not good or bad, just simply as they are. It can take a huge leap of consciousness to do that: it really is not that easy to do. We are trained and imbued with a judgemental way of viewing the world from our earliest years, but it is not what someone does, where they work, how they dress or what car they drive that really matters: it is who they really are underneath that counts. Underneath, everyone is an equal being.

If it is true that the Universe is listening, when we judge some-body, even if they are a thousand miles away, that judgement will be ringing its way out across the ether and will somehow find its way to causing harm. If you always spoke about other people as though they were standing right next to you, how might you change what you are saying about them? Be aware that you don't even have to express a judgement of someone verbally for that person to sense it: they unconsciously feel you judging them.

People whisperers endeavour not to be judgemental of any-one, including themselves and, by doing so, they become good company and lights of attraction. When you communicate with another person and don't judge them, it allows them the freedom to express themselves and be who they really are. This makes it safe for them to speak or act without fear of assessment, reprisal or comeback. When you don't judge people they will be inexplic-ably drawn to you; they will enjoy spending time with you because there is a freedom in your company and you have a lightness about you that is rarely felt or seen.

Things to do:

1. Where are you right now reading this book? Are there any people around? If so, take a look at them now (if not, think back to a recent meeting with a group). What do you think of the people around you? What do you think they are like? How do you know that's true? What effect does thinking that have on your behaviour towards them? Can you look at them with total clarity: completely without judgement?
2. Start to be aware of the ways you judge yourself internally. This can be quite difficult to do in the beginning, because it is so a part of who we think we are that we just don't notice. Pick some obvious examples first, to help you, such as when you find yourself describing yourself as being good or bad at something. Start to notice what self-judgements come out of your mouth: listen to the words you speak and how you use them to judge yourself in front of others and when you are alone.
3. Observe how you label and judge things. Watch other people doing this habitually and see how it gets in the way of clear living and communicating.

4. Experiment with being around people and not judging them at all, even in your mind. You may find yourself going a little quiet – that's because once we drop judgement, even on a subtle level, much of what we normally say becomes irrelevant.

RISKING BEING OPEN

As well as dropping judgement, one of the other ways in which we can enable true communication is by risking being open. In order to experience life in full colour and live life in its full glory, we have to be open. That means being open to the incredible things that life has to offer, such as joy, love, beauty, success, play, laughter, but also being open to hurt, struggle, grief or loss . . . it seems you can't have one without the other!

Generally speaking, the most fun you can have, and some of the worst times you can have, are all to do with the people in your life. It seems that to experience life fully means being open to whatever others bring into your life. Being open is a two-way street: we are open to receive, but also open to give. We can be open to understanding someone else's feelings: and open to sharing our own feelings. We can be open to accepting someone else's reality: and open to sharing our own reality honestly with someone else. We can be open to new experiences, and be open to showing new experiences to someone else.

Sometimes it is as though our soul places us into situations through which it has the best chance of experiencing all that life has to offer, both joyful and painful, and it prises us open, to allow those experiences to flood in. Being open means stepping outside your regular comfort zone, lowering your defences, dropping the familiar secure routine. People who are open are more prepared to face the things they fear most; fortunately, risking being open to feeling more is usually the way to find your greatest gifts, your ultimate freedom and potential. There is only one drawback with accessing your greatest gifts – peace, joy, potential and all – you have to dare go there!

Being Open to Hurt

It is pretty well impossible to go through life without anyone hurting you: to avoid it you would have to live in a very cocooned world of your own, not really letting anyone get close to you or continually withdrawing at the point where things start to feel risky to you. That's fine if that is enough for you, but as human beings we are naturally intimate, sociable and loving creatures who thrive best on interactions with our fellow people. By distancing yourself or staying closed to having someone near to your vulnerable parts, you miss many opportunities. It is really the ego that fears being hurt: the real you, 'who you really are' is impervious to this kind of pain. It is only by taking the risk of losing that we can gain and move forwards.

Sometimes people may hurt you without meaning to or even knowing that they are hurting you: if you let them know that they are hurting you in a non-accusational way, they may be amazed, surprised or sorry . . .

Risking being open does not mean in any way being stupid or reckless with our personal safety, although it can take quite a bit of hammering to crack our shell off if we have grown a very thick and protective version. There may be times when we willingly, desperately want to break out of our protective shell, but we have made it so strong that it takes some kind of major life trauma to crack it open and free us to be our true selves: traumas and difficulties give people a choice to open more to life, or to shrink and close, to protect themselves from a possible repeat of the hurt.

Everything is relative: what may seem comfortable to you may be a very scary degree of 'opening' to someone else. If you know someone who is in the process of breaking out of their shell, it is not always a great idea to be proactive in helping them. People open at the rate and to the extent that they can manage.

Being Open to the New

Being open to the new inevitably means risking the unknown, but without going into the unknown all we will ever do is go around in the same circle, like wearing a groove in the ground where we walk round and round. What happens to most of us, if we walk the same familiar path for too long is that our soul, or fate, bad luck, good luck or just stuff happening – whatever you want to call it – *something* happens to push us out of that safe zone and into changes in life.

It is less costly to move forwards in life by being open than to move forwards by being forced . . . it is actually impossible to stand still in life, but our fear of being open to the new often makes us try to stand still. It would probably be easier for us to fly without wings or walk on water than to make life stand still: let us therefore be open to moving forwards and allow our channels to be open and clear to enable the art of communication to come alive in our lives.

Things to do:

1. Think of areas in which you are afraid to be open, such as your relationships at home or at your work. Now look at other people you know of who are going unharmed into the same areas in their lives as the ones you are afraid of: what is it that they do, say, believe etc. that is different to you and enables them to be open and safe?
2. Think back to a romantic encounter. Did anything hold you back? What would you have said if only you could? Ask yourself how you could allow yourself to express your love more freely.
3. Trust that you will be OK, that the real you cannot be harmed, regardless of how difficult things may be on the surface. Think back to another time in your life when things were difficult or dangerous and acknowledge that you survived to live another day.

Having looked into who you really are and accepted what you found without the need to judge, you have taken a huge first step on the road to discovering the people whisperer within yourself. By this action, you will have begun to expand your ability to communicate with more integrity, openness and honesty, and as you continue with this process of knowing more and more who you really are, your channels of communication will become ever clearer. The next secret of the people whisperer will take this exploration into how you communicate with yourself even further, by tuning in to what your thoughts and feelings are saying.

Secret Two:

Listen to Yourself

EAVESDROPPING ON OUR THOUGHTS

Even if we chat away all day to other people, the first communication we have in any given situation is with ourselves – in the form of our thoughts. Therefore, the way we communicate with ourselves dictates our behaviour and entirely influences the way we communicate with other people. That is why one of the first steps for successful people whisperers is to explore not only our external talking but also our internal 'talking', i.e. what we are thinking.

People whisperers listen to their own thoughts with attention because they know that thoughts go out into the world as speech and action, affecting and influencing everyone around them. Because we don't always express our thoughts out loud, it is easy to think that they happen in some totally secret place inside our brains, but this is not the case. Even on a purely scientific level, thoughts exist as little electro-chemical impulses, so even if our skulls were made of 100 metre-thick insulating concrete, there would be some knock-on effect from them on the outside world. The truth is, it is impossible to have a thought without it being noticed or reflected in some way – even our own bodies 'betray' us by broadcasting our thoughts to the Universe through the subtle signals of body language.

Since the Universe may be listening, perhaps it would be wise to check out what we are communicating to it in our thoughts. That's a bit scary, isn't it? What if the Universe hears some of the rude, crude, hateful, jealous, deceitful, angry, greedy, naughty things we think? Don't worry, we're all doing it; and, anyway, most of us don't truly wish harm to anyone, even to ourselves! Of course, as we become more aware that our thoughts are being broadcast we may choose to think them with more care. Think about the following:

◆ How would you describe the majority of your own thoughts: accepting or judgemental? Helpful or limiting? Confidence-boosting or denigrating? Inspiring or energy-draining? Loving or hateful? Are the majority of your thoughts restricting or enabling?
◆ What effect do you think that your thoughts have on your communications with other people? What effect do they have, for example, on your loved ones, your colleagues and even the environment at large?
◆ Have you inherited your way of thinking about your work, your skills, your money or your life from anyone? If so, who? Has that way of thinking been helpful or detrimental in the long run?
◆ What thoughts would you like to broadcast to the Universe? What are your thoughts telling or asking the Universe right now?

As you continue to eavesdrop on your thoughts, read through the two lists below. Which column would your thoughts mostly fall into?

I just *can't* lose weight.	I just might buy a chocolate factory.
I'm useless at that.	I'll have a go.
Work is such a drag.	Work is great: I get a break from the kids
I am always too tired to enjoy myself.	I'm off out again!
He makes me feel really useless.	He has a need to prove himself.
Where can I find the money from?	Money always finds me when I need it.

She is so pushy and rude.	She has an unfortunate way, poor girl.
Oh, my bum looks big in this.	I am a living Renoir painting!
I wish I was good at something.	I'm about to discover my real talents.
Every time I try that, it's a disaster.	I've learned quite a lot from results.
I never meet the right kind of people.	I'm highly selective about friends.
Business deals always fail on me.	I'm an adventurous entrepreneur; would you like to invest in this brilliant new idea I have for a world-beating company?

As people whisperers, we need to take real notice of our thoughts and our ways of thinking. This doesn't mean that we have to force ourselves to change what we are thinking, or tell ourselves what we should be thinking. By simply noticing our thoughts as we have them, we will begin to take away a lot of the power that unhelpful or destructive thoughts have over us. We also need to be aware that the majority of our thoughts are simply the result of our programming or childhood conditioning; they are not really *us*.

Janet's Story

Janet is a very good doctor in a busy and demanding general practice surgery, but she didn't realise just how much her self-talk – the things she said to and thought about herself – made her life more difficult than it needed to be. So much of her conversation was filled with self-judgement about how she 'should' do this or 'should' do that, or how she wasn't very good at this or that.

Although she was a very attractive, intelligent and caring woman of thirty-five, she had never been in a serious relationship. She often talked

21

about her longing for a meaningful relationship, but at the same time she said she'd probably never meet the man of her dreams. And, even if she did, she said he probably wouldn't be interested in her anyway. Her logic went that as no one suitable had wanted her so far, why should anyone want her now or in the future?

Janet had quite a few hobbies, at all of which she was very accomplished, which was great – except that it gave her even less time in her already busy schedule to stop and relax. She played the flute in a number of amateur orchestras; she painted in watercolours; she worked out at the gym and she loved rowing. But even with respect to her hobbies she was tough on herself: rather than enjoying what she did as pastimes, she had high expectations of doing her hobbies as well as a professional might do them.

At one of our coaching sessions I said to her that it must be really hard to live her life as Janet; that, going by the things she thought and said, she really didn't make it easy for herself to have an nice time and that she put a lot of pressure on herself. I didn't think more about this comment until she came back from a much-needed walking holiday in France and said, 'While I was away I was thinking about what you said: you're right, it is not easy being me and living my life, and I am hard on myself.' It had taken a week of slowing down and having the space to step back from her routine life, for Janet to be able to listen to her self-talk and realise how it made her life so difficult. She looked quite different as a result of this revelation and became very much more aware of how she had judged and pushed herself: she even stopped saying 'I should' all the time, although it occasionally slipped out! Her new-found ability to listen to herself has enabled her to start making some liberating and exciting decisions about the kind of life she wants to create for herself, accompanied by a new sense of lightness.

Things to do:

1. Take the time to listen to yourself – the things you think and say – as often as possible. You don't need to judge, change, justify, analyse or respond – just listen with objective interest to your own inner chatter. At first do this in quiet moments; then practise so that you can do it in challenging situations such as when you are having

a heated or an emotional exchange with someone else. Watch what happens.

2. See if you can trace the origin of some of your thoughts. Who was it that first introduced a particular idea or way of thinking to you? Write down or acknowledge in your mind who the originator of the thought might have been. See how you are freed from unhelpful thoughts once you know they're not the real 'you'.

3. Begin to notice other people's limiting thought patterns through the things they say. (But resist the temptation to point out their self-limiting patterns to them unless they ask you.) In what ways do you do the same thing?

4. Notice the sort of constructive thought patterns that successful, joyful and loving people have through the positive things they say. How might it help you to copy them in some ways?

5. Take note of how life or the universe seems to respond to whatever you communicate to it. For example, have you ever wished ill or anger to someone, then stubbed your own toe, banged your own head, cut your finger on the bread knife or created some other expression of self-inflicted pain? Similarly, have you ever felt quietly lucky about something and it comes up trumps for you? Have you ever thought how nice it'd be to have a certain thing in your life and some time later you get it?

WATCHING YOUR EMOTIONS

As well as being aware of our thoughts, being aware of our emotions is another valuable people-whispering skill. This means consciously and objectively noticing what emotion we are experiencing as we feel it. Taking responsibility for our own emotional states and observing our emotions with interest is an important key to knowing ourselves and thus being better able to connect successfully with other people.

More often than not, our emotions are triggered off by our interactions with the people in our lives. Certain people seem to have the ability to 'set off' stronger emotions in us than others, and it is often those who are closest to us who can affect us most powerfully. When we live fully in the flow of society, relationships, work and all that goes with this, we can certainly feel some stuff! And some of it can be very challenging . . . In the course of one day, we might feel love for a partner or family; miserable at having to get out of bed; uplifted by a great song on the radio; frustrated at sitting in traffic; pleased because someone flirted with us; happy to be welcomed home with a smile . . . The list goes on and on and on! The extraordinary thing is, we all feel this almost constant stream of changing emotions, but most of the time we don't even notice it.

Some people experience their emotions in more extreme measures than others; the highs and the lows being more intense. This is neither good nor bad. We can become addicted to feeling certain emotions – and not just the good ones, surprisingly – and we may start to seek them out as though they are some kind of drug. In one sense, the idea of emotions being a drug is true, since emotions trigger our bodies to release various hormones and chemicals into our systems.

Exploring your emotions

- Who decides how you feel? Who is in control of your emotions: yourself or someone else? And are you in control of your emotions or are they in control of you?
- Do your emotions ever 'run away with you'? Do you like feeling all the emotions you feel, or are some good and some bad? What or who causes you to feel strong emotions?
- Do your emotions ever get in the way of your enjoying life? For you to have a more fulfilled life, which emotions would you like to experience more of? For you to have a more fulfilled life, which emotions would you like to experience less of?

'Control Yourself for Once!'(Well, If You Think It Will Help)

Riding on an emotional roller-coaster requires a huge amount of energy and can also make us react to other people in ways that hinder our effective communication with them. Therefore, it may be helpful to experience our emotions on a more even keel whenever possible.

An important people-whispering step towards balancing our emotions is similar to the one we have already come across with respect to our thoughts, and that is simply to observe how we feel as we feel it. This can have the effect of changing the experience immediately, so that instead of being rattled along on the emotional roller-coaster, we begin to watch our emotions as observers (while feeling and expressing our emotions at the same time). For example, if we were exasperated by someone close, we would simply watch our heated feelings and think, 'Hmm, that's interesting, look how – *aarrgh* - I am feeling about that!' Or maybe we are excited when someone we find attractive walks in the room: we would notice our pulse start racing and our head go fuzzy and think, 'Well, look how *mm-mm-mm* and warm I am getting in the presence of that person . . .!'

It is only with practise that we can truly decide not to feel anger, for example, and just let our rage subside and go away. Actually, enforced 'control' of emotions is not necessarily the best thing to do anyway, as, if we control anything by force, it has a habit of bottling up and then bursting out with real destructive power in some other way.

Whose Emotions Are They?

True people whisperers do not attempt to make others feel a certain way or believe they have permission to determine anyone else's feelings. Nor do people whisperers think that other people are responsible for making them feel how they feel. This can be a hard thing to accept, especially when we're busy blaming someone else for making us feel low, lonely or useless, e.g. 'she makes me feel useless at that' or 'he makes me lose self-confidence in my driving when he is in the car' etc. None of us is likely to let a neighbour choose the colour of our sofa or a work colleague choose our spouse, yet we'd readily accept that other people decide our feelings for us! Therefore, we need to stop and ask ourselves just who is creating our emotions. Who decides how we feel – ourselves or someone else? This is a crucial step to take.

Emotions can motivate or limit us

Some emotions are fantastic for getting us into action. Great speakers through history have stirred their followers' emotions in times of war, for example. We can all use uplifting and motivating emotions to achieve and move forwards in life by guiding our energies and efforts in order to be more inspiring people for others to be around, as well as for inspiring ourselves to achieve more. Not all emotions or emotional reactions are helpful, however, and some can definitely hold us back from being the person we want to be or from connecting with others in the way we would like. Focusing on, and strengthening, our positive emotions such as joyfulness and optimism can make us far easier for other people to be around.

Habitual Emotions

- Do you habitually experience any particular types of emotion? Do you often feel angry, frustrated, afraid or needy? If this is happening to you, begin to notice what patterns are forming and what triggers the habitual emotion.
- Reflect on what ways you either benefit from or lose out by allowing yourself to experience these emotions habitually. Remember that merely recognising the pattern is the first step towards liberating yourself from it.
- Whenever the emotion arises, notice it with objective interest, like a zoologist observing interesting behaviour in an animal through binoculars. As we have seen, noticing when something arises is a way of breaking the hold it has over you.

Extreme emotions

We all know how powerful emotions can be. They can make a man die for love. They can make people kill in anger. They can make nations turn into genocidal maniacs. If extreme emotions are stirred up, it is usually easy to observe them; quite honestly, it is impossible to ignore them! Let's face it, when we are over-whelmed by feelings of being in love, seething with anger, feeling overwhelmed with joy or paralysed by fear, we have no chance of pretending it is not happening within us.

Because of the strength of extreme emotions, controlling them is obviously not so easy, so it can be beneficial to allow them to rise up and run their course, ideally without causing anyone harm, rather than attempt to contain them. If we can observe the emotions at the same time, all well and good.

Things to do:

1. Observe how you feel! What are you feeling while you read this book? What did you feel first thing this morning? What makes you feel that way?

2. Begin to take note of what 'sets you off' into particular emotional states. When someone or something 'makes' you feel a certain way, recognise it and acknowledge it to yourself. This is a hugely liberating and powerful act.

3. Take on board the idea that no one else can really *make* you feel a certain way without you giving them permission to do so.

4. Notice which emotions enhance your time with loved ones, friends or in work situations. Similarly start to notice which emotions detract from those relationships. Are there any emotions that are particularly pleasurable? Are there any that are overwhelming or potentially destructive?

5. Watch other people and see how their emotions either improve or spoil their progress in life. Do the fulfilled people in your life show their emotions. If so, what are they?

6. Be aware when extreme negative emotions are running away with you. Allow them to run their course in a safe way, but continue to be conscious of what is happening as much as possible.

FEAR AND GUILT

Without doubt, fear and guilt are two of the most limiting emotions as far as the people whisperer is concerned and, as such, deserve a special mention. As well as holding us back in all kinds of ways, fear and guilt can also be used as a means for people to control one another and make it more difficult for them to be who they really are. It is the way of the people whisperer, therefore, to be aware of the relationships and behavioural patterns created by fear and guilt, and to choose to be untouched by them. This is sometimes easier said than done, as there may be people in our lives who easily make us feel fear and guilt. Even worse, we may even know people who *try* to make us feel fear or guilt for their own ends, to derive energy from us or to gain control or power over us. But, difficult though it may be, and it's sometimes seemingly impossible, every time we feel fear or guilt we have a choice as to whether we allow these testing emotions to control us or not.

Managing Fear

The type of fear we are talking about here is not physiological – not fear as a reaction to a real danger, such as the fear of being eaten by a lion if, by some bizarre set of circumstances, you find yourself in the lion's enclosure at the zoo! Fear is not always something we can remove from a situation, but what we can do is to find ways to function despite it.

It is important to acknowledge fear when it is present, as by acknowledging it we shine light on it. The light can then show us the way forwards and we can progress despite the fear, by making a leap of faith or by trusting. Fear is an anxious state created by the anticipation of pain or hurt. It may be that the anticipated pain or hurt doesn't actually happen, yet we will have still harmed ourselves and expended energy by feeling the fear of it psychologically anyway. It is not uncommon for our un-founded fears to 'inter-fear' with our behaviour and how we act around people, thus holding us back from comfort and success.

Suggestion

If you find yourself becoming fearful or anxious about a particular person, meeting or interaction, do the following:

- If possible, wait and take a moment to settle yourself inside before interacting with them.
- Calmly observe the breath going in and out of your body.
- Focus your thoughts on a sense of inner stillness.
- When you feel ready take action. Trust yourself!

Fear that blocks communication

When it comes to communicating with other people, our fears can stand in the way of our saying what we think or feel, or what needs to be said. We fear how the other person may react if we say what we would like to say, so instead of expressing it, we hold back. Sometimes this may be a kind or wise thing to do if what we have to say is not necessary and may harm the other person, but sometimes things need to be expressed for the sake of truth, clarity and openness.

Often, our fear of how someone is going to react is far greater than their actual reaction. Alternatively, we may hold back from fear and fail to express ourselves until it is too late, which is a shame for both parties. If you can let someone know that you are only voicing how you feel and not necessarily airing opinions about them, you may find it easier to say your piece, since the person you are talking to will know that they are not on the receiving end of a personal criticism.

Freedom from Guilt

The power of guilt to dominate and control people has long been recognised as a useful weapon by some societies and organised religions: they have often used it not to control or overpower their enemies, but, bizarrely, to hold power over their own followers.

Guilt has been created by people to control people. Nature doesn't feel guilt. When a leopard kills a zebra, when a whale scoops up a whole shoal of fish in one mouthful, when a savage winter decimates the countryside, even when a fox kills every bird in the henhouse but only eats one, nature doesn't indulge in feeling guilty and saying 'Oh, I'm so bad'. It just carries on moving forwards and continues to create more incredible beauty and abundance.

Who is making you feel guilty?

In truth, we are the only people who can make ourselves feel guilty – no one else can do the job for us. Other people can say things in an attempt to trigger our feelings of guilt, but they cannot *make* us feel guilty unless we allow them to.

If we feel guilty about things we have said or done, perhaps now would be a good time to tell ourselves that nobody is perfect and we all do or say things that aren't ideal sometimes. While it may be a constructive thing to recognise when we have done something unreasonable, harmful or thoughtless, it is not constructive to keep replaying it and beating ourselves up over it for ever. Moreover, as we give ourselves permission not to feel guilty, it will be less easy for people to 'run us' by pressing our guilt buttons, since the buttons will not trigger a reaction any more.

If there are other people in our lives (or there have been any previously in our lives) whom we feel ought to feel guilty about things they have said or done to us, we have to realise that our ways of thinking may not be doing them any damage, but they are doing us harm. (We are the ones still being chewed up by negative emotions.) So what would it take to let them – and us – off the hook?

Things to do:

1. Explore your fears. Think of specific people or situations you feared in the past and that turned out to be fine in the end. Go back as far as your earliest years, if you can. Brainstorm a list of all the things you are afraid of, from the big to the very small and write them all

down. Really indulge yourself and get everything off your chest. Bringing your fears out into the open by writing them down is a liberating technique to begin to free you from their grip.

2. If there is someone you are afraid of, intimidated by or apprehensive about, put yourself in their position and see if you can understand what makes them behave in a way that scares you. Could it be that they themselves are terrified of something? If you are in a fearful place about someone, ask yourself what options you have when dealing with them in the future: come up with at least three options, regardless of how outlandish they may seem.

3. Do you ever find yourself not communicating to your loved one for fear of saying or doing the wrong thing? Do you ever find yourself trying to imply what you want to say, rather than saying it in a clear, straightforward way – almost as though you are still trying to say it, but hiding it at the same time? Think back to a recent time when you wanted to say something but stopped yourself, through fear. How might events have turned out differently if you had said what was on your mind then? How can you really know unless you give it a go? Come up with a best-case scenario.

4. What things might you have done in your life if fear hadn't stopped you? What things would you do if fear wasn't stopping you now? What things would you do with the rest of your life if there was no fear? Make a wish list for the future.

5. Write down a list of the main things you feel guilty about. Next to each thing, write how long you think it would be constructive to keep beating yourself up about it. Then next to that, in a third column, write down what positive benefit you gain from feeling guilty about it. Now do what nature does: tear up your list, drop the guilt and move forwards to a new day and the coming of the next season.

6. Become observant of how other people use fear and/or guilt to control you: once you see how this is happening, you have a conscious choice about whether or not to allow them to continue controlling you, even if you have to take the drastic measure of removing them from your life or removing yourself from their's.

7. Write a list of all the people you think should feel guilty for what they did to you. If you can, think of a positive reason why they might have done what they did to you. Think of something you may have learned

from their treatment of you. Their behaviour and, in many cases, they themselves, may no longer exist in your life; they only exist in your memory. So read through the names and thank each one of them, tell them you forgive them and tell them it is now time for you to let them go.

Having explored the people whisperer's second secret, we can see more clearly how the ways in which we communicate with ourselves through our thoughts and feelings impact upon our whole lives, and most particularly in our interactions with other people. Simply by noticing what is happening, without even attempting to alter anything consciously, we will have expanded our ability to understand and connect with those around us. Secret Three will take this exploration even further, by utilising another of our natural resources: our body.

Secret Three:

Trust Your Body

People whisperers know that our physical body is one our greatest attributes and allies: it is an integral and physical manifestation of who we are and constantly guides us as to the right course of action and the right companions to share our lives with. Our bodies give us constant, moment-to-moment feedback about how we feel, what we think and the ways in which we are interacting with our environment and the people in it: the body is truly a part of who we are.

Our bodies are always looking out for us, whispering information that will help us in so many ways, if we are able to listen. Unfortunately, we only really listen to our bodies when they start giving us information we cannot ignore, normally in the form of aches, pains, disease, bursts of joy or sexual excitement. The rest of the time, our bodies are nevertheless doing their best to tell us what is going on, but we seldom listen.

WHAT IS YOUR BODY TELLING YOU?

Like the skin of a chameleon that changes colour in response to its environment, so, too, our bodies change in response to our environment. Every cell in the body reflects our thoughts and emotions, affording us a fabulous source of information about what is happening in our lives and how we feel about the people around us. Have you ever noticed how some people make you feel 'uncomfortable' and some make you feel 'comfortable'? This is an example of your body giving you feedback. Other ways in which our bodies give us feedback are by telling us what kinds of food are right for us and what exercise is appropriate for us.

The Body Does Not Lie

Our bodies carry a blueprint of all we have ever thought, felt or been through in our lives. Unlike our minds and mouths, which can hide the truth even from ourselves, the body responds at a deeper and therefore more honest level. You may tell yourself, for example, that you don't feel anxious about meeting your boss, but your body will know the truth and have the jitters regardless of your apparent mental stance. You may tell yourself that you don't find a particular person attractive, but again if this is not true, your body may inform you otherwise! Our bodies respond to different people in so many different ways.

It is important to realise that the body gives us feedback the whole time, not just in major situations. The different ways our bodies react are often very subtle, but if we are aware of these reactions we can use this information as a guide in our communication with other people.

Here are a few examples of ways our bodies can give us feedback:

◆ When we feel insecure, unsafe or defensive the body tends to 'close up'. We may cross our legs, fold our chests in a little, drop our eyes away from whoever we are with and fold our arms across our chests. Internally, our joints and internal muscles may tighten slightly, heart and breathing become less relaxed and stomach (solar plexus) tighten when we feel this way.

◆ If we are anxious or nervous the heart rate will usually increase; the breathing becomes shallow; the stomach may churn and the body tenses in preparation for fight or flight. We may feel sick and our throats close slightly; our legs may feel wobbly, our eyes flit about or look tense and startled, and our bowels may feel loose (hopefully not too loose!).

◆ If we feel comfortable or loving towards someone the whole body will usually feel more at ease. The stomach, muscles and joints relax and the chest expands (in Eastern tradition this corresponds with the heart chakra opening). We take on a relaxed and friendly posture, spreading out to take up more space and our eyes soften.

◆ If we feel excited or full of fun we often have a sense of the body expanding and our faces literally open up in smiles and laughter. We may feel as though we actually weigh less as the body moves with more freedom and release. Heart rates may be a bit quicker than usual, but in a healthy aerobic way rather than pumping the fight or flight hormone, adrenalin, round our body.

◆ If the person we are with makes us feel sexually excited, well ... most of us will have noticed what our bodies feel like in that situation already!

The neck

The neck is a narrow channel between the head, where most of the 'thinking' takes place, and the body, where most of the 'doing' takes place. The neck therefore carries a lot of information about our reactions to whatever is going on in any given situation, with tension in the neck inhibiting the flow of information between the brain and the body. One of the reasons that bodywork practices such as the Alexander technique are so useful is because they work at releasing tension in the neck.

It is certainly interesting to see how different people carry their heads in different ways upon their shoulders ...

Tune in to Your Body

To become aware of how every single thought has a reaction in the body, sit comfortably and quietly with your eyes closed and think of someone or something that you find really relaxing and peaceful. Feel how your body softens and relaxes, your heart slows and your stomach lets go.

Now think of a person or situation you have to face that is scary or challenging: what happens to your body? Most likely it starts getting tense, stomach knotting and heart speeding up.

Acknowledging the Feeling

There is so much to be gained from simply listening to the body and observing what it is doing. As we saw with respect to thoughts and feelings in Secret Two, observation alone can be hugely beneficial. Sometimes simply noticing a reaction and recognising that we have noticed the body's message will help us to manage a situation better.

Acknowledge the feeling in your body by consciously giving your attention to it, almost as though you were an interested onlooker: this takes some of the power away from your reaction and can put you back in control of a situation, since you then have the choice to respond, rather than react.

If we wait for the body to start metaphorically 'yelling' something at us before we take notice of it, it may have already entered a state that will actually increase the difficulty of a situation, making us more tense, nervous, angry or frightened.

If we listen to our own bodies when we are with other people, this will tell us a great deal about them. It may tell us whether they are coming from the heart or not. In this way, the information the body gives us can act as an early warning radar, helping us to prevent situations and relationships from becoming more hazardous or difficult than they need to be.

Fiona's Story

To begin with, Fiona loved her new job: not only did she enjoy what she did, but it gave her the opportunity to live in the countryside, since the post she had found came with a cottage attached. She was also able to keep her horse there too, and it was the first time she had ever been in such a lucky position. Fiona didn't even have to travel to work any more: her employer's home, the main house on the estate, was also the centre for his business. It all seemed to fit perfectly.

From time to time through her life, Fiona had experienced bouts of eczema and asthma. When I first met her she had been in her new job for about three months, by which time her eczema and asthma had re-appeared and was becoming increasingly worse. Before long, she was in constant discomfort and forced to seek the advice of specialists. As well as following a very pure diet, she was given a prescription in order to control her raging symptoms, but nothing appeared to work. It seemed more than coincidental that her ailments had worsened so significantly since moving to her new place and job, and so I asked Fiona if perhaps her body was trying to tell her something.

Fiona is a very amenable, gentle and sensitive person, in contrast to her employer, who was sometimes very difficult to deal with. He was a loud, controlling, even bullying man, who would fly off the handle at the slightest upset, not caring what he said or who was on the receiving end of his tantrums. After putting up with this for nearly two years, Fiona had become quite worn out by tip-toeing her way through the daily minefield created by this atmosphere of fear and intimidation, and so she finally found another job to go to.

Within days of moving away from her old job and home, Fiona experienced an almost miraculous recovery from her eczema and asthma. It has been said that eczema is caused by intense irritation and that asthma is caused by things being suppressed and not said. Both of these descriptions fit perfectly with Fiona's previous situation: because of fearing the temperamental reactions of her boss, quite understandably, she constantly suppressed what she wanted to say and, as such, she lived in a state of permanent irritation in his vicinity. Had Fiona listened to her body sooner, she may have realised that her body was shouting a message to her, that the situation she had placed herself in was not good for her and that it wanted her to get out of there. Her body had been letting her know for nearly two years that she needed to move away from the situation, and thankfully she had moved in the end. These days Fiona often mentions the messages she ignored at that time and now listens very attentively to her body all the time.

Things to do:

1. Stop reading this for a moment and scan your attention down through your body right now: go from your head, jaw, tongue, to your neck, shoulders, guts, lower spine, seat, legs and arms. Notice if there is a pocket of tension of which you hadn't been aware. Can you release it? You probably won't have to shake yourself about or make any big movements in order to release it; most likely you simply have to 'allow' it to soften.

2. Sit in a relaxed state and think about a person or situation that makes you really anxious or frightened. Listen to what your body tells you in response to merely thinking about the situation. Repeat this process until you can think vividly about the person or situation without your body reacting at all.
3. Sitting comfortably, breathe deeply and allow your body to relax. Now think in depth about various people in your life, one at a time. See what your body tells you in response to your thoughts about each person.
4. See if you can become aware of your whole body as a complete entity. Stay with this for a moment and be aware of how it feels. The next time that you talk to someone, see what happens if you focus on experiencing your whole body as a single entity during your conversation. Scan through your body to see what it is doing, feeling or telling you while the conversation takes place.

WATCH YOUR BODY TALK

As well being a great source of information about ourselves, our bodies play a large part in our communications with other people. Figures vary, but it is generally agreed that less than 50 per cent of communication is done via the spoken word. The successful people whisperer is therefore aware of the messages that his or her body communicates to others and is likewise attuned to other people's body language on both the physical and the subtle levels, so that he or she 'hears' much more than just the spoken word. Mastering body language is a skill that enables people whisperers to respond to situations perceptively and intuitively, and to interact with others in an understanding, effective and appropriate way.

As we have seen, our bodies' thoughts and emotions are intrinsically linked. As well as registering what our bodies tell us about our environment, it is also possible to send traffic the other way: that is, by deliberately influencing the body's actions, we can consciously communicate, convey information, influence, change or manage our emotions and the way we feel. For example, if you take up a dominant and powerful stance with your body like Schwarzenegger does in the movie *Terminator*, the pose will probably make you feel powerful, solid and grounded (even though other people may snigger). It is quite difficult to feel small, insecure and weak in this position. On the other hand, were you to take up a body posture associated with timid and closed emotional states, your feelings would probably follow suit. Likewise, it would be quite difficult to feel miserable when smiling, jumping up and down and waving your arms up in the air.

What we are talking about here goes way beyond external body language. External body language can express certain attitudes or messages to others, but if the internal body state is expressing something different to the external body language, we are not being fully effective; whereas if the internal body state matches the external body language, we can become highly expressive, powerful and focused.

Infinite Ways to Express

Once we have begun to listen to our bodies and have an increased awareness of what they are saying to us and about us, there are an infinite number of ways we can use them to express ourselves and influence the nature of our interactions with other people. Here are some pointers:

◆ **To appear nonchalant**, take up a casual, open posture, lowering your heart rate, sighing and focusing on inner relaxation.
◆ **To appear determined**, take up a firm stance that enables you to feel more solid inside and out.
◆ **To appear unthreatening**, allow softness into your face and body, rest one leg and centre yourself inwardly.
◆ **To appear completely unstoppable**, focus your eyes to the horizon, feel firm but not fixed inside, and raise yourself up physically.
◆ **To project an air of unconditional love and acceptance** (very worth while in many situations), relax your stomach muscles and take gentle, slow breaths. Give your full attention to the other person; let your mind and body be still. Feel centred in your torso.

To begin with, it can feel strange to play around with your body posture and movement, but soon it may become good fun! In the same way that a dictionary is full of words we rarely use, there are many means of physical expression that our bodies are capable of, but which we don't normally employ. Using new words may feel clumsy until we integrate them into our everyday vocabulary, and sometimes we might even use them in the wrong context (much to the amusement of those around us). The same applies when using our bodies in new ways as a means to express ourselves: skill comes with practice and the whole process begins with body awareness.

The Power in Your Body

When our bodies are fully aligned with our thoughts, intentions and emotions, our actions become highly effective. The body becomes such a powerful tool for expression, that we can give out seemingly tiny signals and yet achieve big results. However, if the body is not truly aligned with the rest of us – our inner selves – it may perform all manner of huge and laboured actions to little effect. In this context, the term 'aligned' means that the mind, body and intention are in agreement and all these aspects of us are focused on a common goal. Our bodies then become the physical manifestation, the tip of the iceberg, of all those inner resources in action. This is how great sports-people can achieve such feats: their bodies are powered by the combined strength of their wills, their minds, their intentions and their inner energies. When such focus is expressed with commitment the results can be outstanding and seemingly effortless.

We can use the same level of alignment to perform feats of incredible stillness too; if we let our bodies become physical representations of inner stillness and peace, this will give the appearance that we are untouchable. This can have a very calming effect in heated situations, almost as though the body becomes a fire blanket, damping down the flames of the exchange.

This idea of alignment and the fact that our bodies speak the truth is useful when we are around other people. You can surely think back to an occasion when you were with someone who was doing something apparently very loving and giving, but the feeling your body got from being near the other person's body did not match the other's actions. Similarly, you may recall being with someone who was saying or doing something apparently offensive, but somehow your body said it was OK and the other person's body was not giving a threatening feeling in the same way as their actions. When someone speaks with congruence, their body is naturally aligned with their message; when someone speaks with duplicity, their body is naturally inclined to show it and as people whisperers we will increasingly be able to sense when this is the case.

PEOPLE WATCHING

As we have already seen, much of what other people communicate to us is expressed through their bodies. We have all learned the body language we use; we weren't born with it. Proof of this is to be found in the way that teenagers acquire a different way of standing and moving when they hang around with other teenagers on the block. What was a perfectly good posture and walk for a child is uncool for a teen: they have to learn to walk like the latest movie star or rapper dude.

Noticing other people's bodies and what they are expressing is as interesting as studying your own body: have a look and listen to what people's bodies are saying about them and about the messages they are conveying to the world. We can often tell how someone is feeling or what they are thinking merely by observing their posture and body language. Once we have noticed another person's state we have far more choice about whether to be affected by their emotions or not. We will also have more insight into what might be the right thing to say to them at that time (or whether it may be wiser to keep quiet and not say anything!).

When we listen to our own bodies, much of the information is internal: feelings in different parts of our bodies. Where other people are concerned, much, but not all, of the information we receive is external. Some of the ways people express themselves with their bodies are quite blatant: but aside from the obvious messages conveyed by people's bodies, there are usually many other subtle messages involved and it is fascinating to listen to these.

Suggestion

The next time you have a conversation take a good look at whoever you are talking to while they speak:

- Watch their eyes change as the things they talk about change. Do their eyes shine out with light or are they dull? Do their eyes flit about or are they restful and able to look at you? Do they convey love or mistrust? The eyes are said to be the windows of the soul: when you look into someone's eyes, what do you see of them?
- When they smile, do their eyes smile along with their mouth or do they not give much away?
- Is their mouth and jaw relaxed or tight? Do they open their mouth and speak their truth freely, or do they talk through a half-closed mouth, as though their words don't matter or are maybe not true?
- Watch how they sit, stand and move. What do they do with their body mass? Do they move in a centred way or apologetically, in a nervous or agitated way, or do they appear confident and calm?
- Does their head and shoulder position look light and floating, or heavy and weighed down by life? Do their shoulders look rounded and worn, or proud and strong?
- What speed are their movements? Do they have to fiddle with things and keep adjusting themselves or do they have a comfortable inner stillness about them?

The aura

We could explore external physical signals for a long time, but there is another level at which we can listen to another person's body. This level concerns the sort of subliminal presence and energy that someone brings with them when they enter a room; it is the 'atmosphere' they carry within and around them. Some people may equate this to the aura. It's perhaps debatable whether auras exist in the literal sense (I've never seen one but that doesn't mean they aren't there!), but however sceptical we may be about them, every person we meet definitely has a different kind of energy charge to them. This charge, feeling, energy, aura or whatever you want to call it is quite tangible and is a valuable source of information for us in our communication. Therefore, the people whisperer remains receptive to auras or their equivalent when in company.

Things to do:

1. Explore ways to support your communications by using your body in different ways, using the suggestions listed above. For example, practise having a 'bigger', louder physical presence and then having a 'smaller', quieter physical presence. Make a note of how changing your body language affects your emotions or self-confidence.
2. Start to notice how you walk, stand and sit. What does your posture say about you? Is your body language open or closed, receptive or intimidating?
3. Pay attention the next time you meet someone to what that person does with their facial expressions, hands and body when they are talking to you. Pay attention to what your face, hands and body do when you are talking to them.
4. Stand and look at yourself in a full-length mirror: what stance do you naturally take? What kind of person would you guess someone is, if you met them and they had your posture? Play around with the variety of ways you can express with your body. See how tiny changes in the mirror make a real difference to what is being expressed.
5. Next time you are talking to someone, allow your subtle 'inner' body to listen to the other person's subtle 'inner' body. What kind of experience does that give you?

In the past three Secrets, we have explored how we communicate internally with ourselves through our thoughts, emotions and judgements, getting a sense of who we really are. We have also seen what a great ally, tool for expression and source of information our own bodies are. And we have seen how other people's bodies speak volumes too. Now that we have begun to master the secrets of communicating effectively with ourselves, the time has come to take a closer look at the ways in which we communicate with others – people whispering in practice.

PART II

People Whispering In Practice

Secret Four

Hold the Space

Successful people whisperers are self-aware at every level – mentally, emotionally and physically. This self-awareness applies in all forms of communication, but especially in the quality of the way that they listen.

TRULY LISTENING

Listening is one of the foundation stones for effective communication, and to truly listen means to absorb what that person is saying with the whole self – body, mind and soul. Spoken words that enter through our ears are only one aspect of listening. To take the quality of our listening to a deeper level, we can make our whole body into an open, receiving, listening device. This doesn't necessarily involve words or sounds, but it does mean allowing our body to be still and to receive whatever type of energy comes from another person.

In physical terms, when we listen with our whole body we have a sense of the front of our body – our chest or stomach – opening out towards the person who is talking. This receptive state gives us a sense of what is being expressed that is beyond words, so that we absorb much of what is being communicated without having to analyse it. This means that we learn a huge amount about someone: far more than what is said through their words alone.

Truly listening is one of the ultimate loving acts we can perform and one of the most powerful forms of exchange that can take place between people. Sometimes people just need to talk, to be free to offload whatever is going on for them. When we truly listen to someone, we give them a gift beyond words, because our listening offers them a safe space in which to express themselves. It may even help them to see things in ways they never saw before or help them to explore areas of themselves or their lives that they haven't been to before. In this way, truly listening can be like healing given by the listener to the person talking.

How to Truly Listen

When we are truly listening, we are calm and patient, and sense when it is appropriate for us to speak, if we need to speak at all. The state of quiet and inner stillness that we adopt when we really listen means that we don't justify, sort out, compare, judge or discard anything that is said. We intuitively know the right question to ask or the right thing to say. (Though that doesn't necessarily mean that we have to agree with what is being said!)

Truly listening means that we don't give our opinion or tell someone what they *should, shouldn't* or *ought* to do, and, we become so present-moment focused that we suspend awareness of time. Our mind is so quiet that we don't have any emotions mounting inside us that could interfere with our listening. This means that we don't need to find solutions for the other person by coming up answers to their dilemmas. Only they can discover the answers that are right for them, but our high-quality listening will help them in their discovery.

It is essential that we do not alter the words or the meaning of the words spoken by someone else: they have chosen those words for a reason, though that choice may be unconscious. Because truly listening means that we give someone our full attention, it is important that we don't do anything else at the same time: it is best to put aside anything else and simply listen. Nor do we need to keep interjecting with comments to prove that we are still listening.

Listening with your body

We have seen that when we listen with our whole body we feel as though the front of our body is opening out towards the person who is talking. (However, if what is being said is disturbing or perhaps harmful to us, instead of opening the front of our body, we can consciously close it up or imagine an invisible screen in front of us to protect ourselves.) To create the effect of truly listening with our body, we can imagine a sense of the space around us and the other person, almost like we are both in an invisible capsule that surrounds and suspends us both, including the space around us. By doing this we open up new possibilities, creating that space and allowing the speaker to fill it with new expressions or ideas. By creating a sense of shared space, we may become very attractive to the other person (not simply in a physical way), because we are giving them something priceless, something that is very rarely given – our full and undivided attention, and permission to talk freely.

Things to do:

1. Experiment with truly listening. Sit or stand quietly, and consciously give someone the level of attention and time they need in order to express themselves to you. Use relaxed, physical stillness of your body as a helpful step towards truly listening: when someone is talking to you, keep your body still, peaceful and comfortable. Allow your energy levels to settle, let go of thinking about the time and give your full attention to the other person.
2. Practise letting go of judgement or internal analysing when some-one speaks to you, in the way that we looked at in Secrets One and Two.
3. Be aware of your entire body while someone is speaking to you; feel the energy in your body and how it is responding to what they are communicating to it . . . (Mmm, could be interesting!).
4. If someone is rambling on, not really engaging their brain with their mouth and is ending up boring the body-parts off you, ask them relevant questions to bring them back on to the course of a con-structive communication.
5. Avoid exploiting the art of truly listening as a means to seek gain or profit for yourself, though you will be amazed at what can come back to you as a result of truly listening.

Holding the Space

Holding the space means being fully present when we are with someone: we give them all the room they need in which to express themselves. We stay in a peaceful state and create a stillness around us, allowing the person to bring whatever they wish to bring or say whatever they need to say. We don't analyse or judge what they say; we listen with the whole of our being, not only to what they are saying with their words, but we also listen to their energy and expression through their essence. Holding the space means that we give someone our full attention inside and out: it is one of the greatest gifts we can give.

The time when we are holding the space is all about them – all about the other person. We are giving them love and respect by being fully there and not attempting to take up any of the space with our own ego or 'stuff'. We have laid aside all of our own worries, ideas, expectations, wants and thoughts for the duration of the time that we are with the other person in this listening mode.

Questions from beyond the mind

When we ask questions whilst holding the space, the questions do not come from our mind: they come from our intuition. We do not think about the question before we ask it; the question comes for the other person out of what they have previously said. This way, the questions we ask – if we do ask them – are always the right questions. Sometimes when we are holding the space we may ask questions that even surprise us as we speak them.

The Gifts of Holding the Space

◆ Holding the space allows all kinds of incredible things to come up for us and for others present.
◆ Holding the space allows for expansion: quite simply, because we are creating more space.
◆ Holding the space makes someone feel totally safe to explore and say whatever they want without fear of reaction: it is

almost as though we hold them in a protective bubble where there is only that person, us and the area surrounding us both. They are protected from anything outside of the bubble and everything inside it is totally non-judgemental and safe too.

◆ Holding the space is the ultimate in high-quality listening: nothing else is going on within us except that. This is what makes it such high-quality listening.

◆ Holding the space often brings about great solutions or learning for someone, but in one sense we have not had to do anything. We have just been there: totally.

The opposite of holding the space is what we do most of the time: we fill every corner of our time and space in our lives with business, with our own stuff – with wanting, pushing, wishing, talking, thinking etc. The space is always there for us to expand into; it is just that we fill it up all the time. Like concreting over the earth, it is there everywhere underneath, but we cover it up.

Things to do:

1. Practise being aware of your own inner space: that is the space taken up by your body and the near surrounding area. Practise sitting on your own and being totally quiet, inside and out.

2. Allow someone to express themselves whilst you give your full, loving, undivided attention: acknowledge their view and accept that their reality is their reality, whether it contrasts with yours (which it would be natural for it to do) or not.

3. Enjoy the two-way feeling of energy that happens when you hold the space for someone: as you allow them the space to expand, so too, you are inevitably expanded, since you are an integral part of what is happening.

Listening to Feedback (Receiving Messages)

'Feedback' is another word for results: the type of results that we receive in the form of information or messages in response to what we put out into the world.

We live in the Information Age, and we receive information constantly – from the Universe, from other people and from our own internal sources (body, mind and soul). The question is: do we notice the information we receive? This is a large part of what people whispering is about: it is not just about how we communicate our messages outwards, but almost more importantly, how receptive we are to what is being communicated inwards to us, from other people, relationships, events and the Universe at large . . . How can we know what to do or say next if we don't listen and really know what is going on for the people around us or in the Universe at large?

Keys to Noticing Feedback

Start noticing what is happening around you: think of your life, the people and relationships and happenings within it all as feedback about whom and how you are being, and what you are doing and communicating.

Tiny signals

Sometimes the messages we receive are very quiet, but we still need to notice them. If we are busy and wrapped up in our own reality, it is easy not to be aware of the tiny signals that are being given to us. It is not uncommon for someone in a relationship to 'suddenly' be left by their partner without any warning. But is it true that there was no warning? Often, people on the outside of the relationship saw it coming because they had noticed the tiny signals.

Quiet, tiny messages can bring good fortune. If we miss them by not listening attentively, we miss the benefit too. Hear what the universe is telling you by what is happening in your life, relationships and the world around you, even in the tiniest signals.

However tiny or large it may be, remember that feedback is simply that: feedback. We may interpret it as criticism, aggression, flattery, underhandedness or any one of a thousand-and-one labels, but by labelling it, we may have already altered the original meaning of the message. And stop denying it! The easiest way to miss valuable feedback is to deny that that is what it is. Everything and anything could be giving us clues that will lead us to the life, relationship, joy, freedom or Holy Grail we wish for, but by choosing to deny the feedback we are being given, by refusing to listen, we will miss the gifts. By not listening to feedback, especially small signals that we are being given, we open ourselves up to receiving much bigger, more painful or sometimes cataclysmic feedback such as major illness, divorce, bankruptcy or even premature death (in an extreme case).

Things to do:

1. Try this exercise: start a conversation with a friend, and when one of you has spoken for a little while, the other person will repeat back what has been said. The interesting thing is how, most often, the repetition of the message from the second person will have been changed so much.
2. Look at what has happened to you today, yesterday or in the last week. View what has happened as feedback: about decisions you have made, things you have said or done and ways you have been.
3. Look for some tiny signals in your life and explore what possible significance they may have.
4. Listen to other people carefully and hear how they filter information in different ways to you. How do they respond or interpret the same information as you? Use these differences to begin to understand how you filter information and how you might filter it in more helpful ways.
5. Base your decisions and responses on the feedback you receive. Let's face it, the feedback you would get by sticking your hand in a fire would alter your responses very quickly, yet unfortunately, we don't learn from other sources of feedback in our lives nearly so quickly!

The Power of Words

Words provide an extraordinary means for us to communicate with each other: they have the power to create or destroy, bring peace or suffering, love or hate. Not only are there a huge number of words available to us, but each word has so many subtle variations of meaning and inflection, giving us an endless range of possibilities for expression. This allows us to take verbal communication to a very advanced level. The people whisperer is therefore aware of the creative and destructive power of words, and chooses words with care, being very attentive to their meaning. The people whisperer also listens to the words people use and what those words convey, both directly and by suggestion, at the conscious and unconscious level.

One drawback created by the wide variety of possibilities that words present to us is the potential for misunderstanding and misinterpretation; this sometimes represents a *massive* challenge, even in close personal relationships, where two people have found a partner with whom they are extremely harmonious.

Words are Also a Way that We Communicate with Ourselves . . .

People whispererers are interested in the unconscious choices we make through the words we use. We often use words and phrases habitually, oblivious to the ways that they may be holding us back or limiting us. It is worth remembering that your unconscious mind listens to and believes in every single word you say. You don't have to say things like you 'can't' do something, you are terrible with money or you always get a broken heart when you fall in love, that many times before your unconscious mind starts believing these statements are true. And once the unconscious believes something to be true, it will affect your behaviour in order to bring what it believes to be the truth into reality. This makes the choice of words, even when communicating to yourself, highly significant.

The people whisperer's glossary

Let's look at some words that are particularly relevant to mastering the secrets of people whispering. (This list is by no means exhaustive!)

Appropriate: This is a very useful word to use when talking to someone about a difficult area of behaviour. By saying we don't feel something is appropriate, we are making a clear statement that it is not suitable behaviour, without sounding like we are accusing or blaming the other person: it is difficult for someone to argue with a statement like 'I don't feel it is appropriate for me'.

Awareness, self-awareness and other-awareness: This means noticing what is going on. If we notice what goes on inside ourselves, emotionally, mentally, physically, then we are self-aware. If we notice those things in others, we are 'other-aware', and if we notice those things in the Universe we are in danger of being referred to as a Guru or crackpot, depending on the viewpoint taken by others!

Boundary: This is a line drawn in the sand, a way of stating to others what is acceptable to us and what is not. It is not a confrontational stance, but a clear message.

Buttons (as in 'pressing'): In this context, the word 'buttons' has nothing to do with undoing your shirt: it means someone getting a reaction from another person (normally an emotional one) by saying or doing a certain thing, their action causing an involuntary reaction in the other person. People close to us can be especially good at pressing our buttons and making us react this way.

Choices: Like making a selection of what we want from a menu, choices are how we decide what we want life to dish out to us, a gourmet feast of incredible, loving, fun experiences or a plateful of indigestible difficulties. This is also about how we decide to respond to the dishes with which we are served and how we decide to feel about them.

Compassion: This is a sense of empathy and love towards someone at a heart level, born from the feeling that, underneath, we and they are the same beings.

Controlling: This means attempting to impose our will on someone else to direct that person and limit the choices that are their natural right. It is a form of behaviour that comes from not trusting in the flow of life and being run by our fears and insecurities.

Empathy: Being empathic means understanding, accepting and identifying with some else's feelings or situation. It is not the same as being sympathetic, which is more akin to feeling sorry for someone and is not particularly empowering for them.

Energy: Everything is made of energy. Eastern religions have been telling us that for thousands of years and, just recently, scientists have caught up and agreed! Everything is filled with energy too: a stone, thin air, our body, our thoughts, love – even couch potatoes have energy. Energy can appear inert or 'apparently' inactive, but it is still present in huge amounts. Think about the amount of energy released by splitting the atom in an atomic bomb; now think how much energy we have contained within our body, which is made up of countless trillions of atoms. Think what we could do if we released that energy and used it for good.

Flow: This is the natural state of everything: the way that it is all meant to happen, freely, easily and without resistance.

Hope: This is often seen as a positive word, e.g. 'Where there's life there's hope.' But 'hope' really does leave plenty of room for things not to turn out right – it is often about handing over power to someone or something else, like luck, for instance.

Intention: Our intention is something we plan to do. It is more positive than 'want to do', 'would like to do' or 'hope to do': intention gives a clear message that we are committed to the arrival of a particular outcome. For example, 'I intend to give up smoking tomorrow' is more powerful than 'I want to try to give up smoking tomorrow'.

Love: This is the most powerful force in existence, it is the material that binds everything in the Universe together. It is inside, outside and around everything, although much of the time we don't notice it, partly because we are also made of it, but more because we are so wrapped up in thinking and doing. When we are aware of love, the feelings of ecstasy, bliss and awe that signify it are, well, ecstatic, blissful and awesome!

No: With only two letters, 'No' is one of the biggest words in our vocabulary. It can be a hard word to hear from someone; it can also be a *very* hard word to say to someone.

Purpose: This is what we are really here for, what we are meant to do with our life and where we can best place our intentions and energy. Once we find our true purpose, all kinds of inner resources and energy will be made available to us.

Pushing: This is when someone tries to use their weight of personality or determination to force an outcome or result. Pushing often creates counter-resistance, i.e. pushing back. It is not a very energy-efficient way of having relationships or achieving goals.

Should(n't): This is a very 'parent-like' word, which carries an implication that if we don't do what we 'should' do, we will be bad or wrong. It is a word that implies a moral judgement and says that our words, actions or events in life are expected to be a certain way, which they usually are not, of course! For example, I *should* be good at doing this by now; you *should* be earning more money; the tenants upstairs *shouldn't* be so noisy when they're having sex during Lent!

Soul: This is our life-energy, the essence of who we really are. It is infinite, untouchable, eternal and divine.

Space: This is the empty, free territory between everything. It is becoming quite rare on earth, both physically and mentally. We tend to fill every available space with thought, word, deed or 'stuff'. Having more space, for however fleeting the moment, allows new insight and fresh possibilities to be created. Although we perceive there to be emptiness between events and objects, it is in fact filled with divine energy or love, as is everything and everywhere. That means that space is also a form of love, if you can figure that one out.

Our use of words also informs other people how we operate, what our beliefs are and in what ways we are self-limiting. If we are an aware and careful listener, we can tell quite a lot – even about someone we have only just met – from hearing them speak a few sentences and noticing their choice of words to describe their reality. If we listen to the words that others use, we will see how their vocabulary is reflected in the kind of life and reality that they create for themselves.

Suggestion

Listen to the words you use and realise how they are creating your reality. Remember that words are very powerful and consequently choose your words with precision.

Boomerang words and actions

One of the reasons why it is important to be aware of what we say is that every word we speak (and every action we take) that relates to other people will come back to us in some way or other. Every thought, word and action has an energy that goes out from us and will ultimately return in some way or other, whether we are conscious enough to recognise it or not. Once we have expressed our words or actions, they are 'out there' and once they are out there we have absolutely no control over them – we can only guess how they will come back. It may often return in a very indirect way, so we would have to be incredibly aware to recognise it.

Much of what we say comes back to us in quite obvious ways: if we express ourselves with love, love will come back; if we express ourselves with violence, violence will come back. If we wish someone well and praise them, even if they are two thousand miles away, some day that good intention will come back to us somehow. Similarly, if we talk about someone in a derogatory way, even if they are a thousand miles away, one day our ill feeling will come back to us somehow. Successful people whisperers know that words and actions always come back like boomerangs, so they flow with this indisputable Universal law in order to create the kind of relationships and experiences they wish to enjoy. They are also aware that just one thoughtless word or action can undo years of building rapport, love and trust, and therefore make thoughtful words and actions one of their routine practices.

Things to do:

1. The next time you have a conversation, notice what words the other person is using. What are they really saying? Start to notice what words you habitually use and what you are really saying.

2. Begin to notice how words not only create the experiences, relationships and happenings in people's lives, but also how the words people use seem to create and shape their personalities and personal characteristics too. Now think about how your words are shaping you. For example, take note of those people whom you meet who use phrases such as 'can't do' a lot and those who use the words 'can do' a lot.

3. Listen to yourself and hear the words you are using: you may sometimes be surprised to hear yourself using words that harm you, put yourself down or give you a negative experience. If you notice any of your words doing this, drop them. It may be better to say less than use words to create hurt or negativity in your life or the lives of your loved ones.

4. Make a commitment to avoid gossiping, especially about other people. Remember the boomerang effect, and that words have the power to heal or to harm, so make sure that, as much as you can, your words are not harming anyone. Explore what happens if you never criticise or speak negatively about anyone whatsoever, whether they are in the vicinity or not. Notice how much people 'bad-mouth' those who are not around to defend themselves.

5. Start sending positive energy out into the world through your words and actions, for example by doing small favours for your friends and family. Do this without being asked and without expecting direct rewards to fly back to you, but watch the results with interest.

6. Whenever someone compliments you, boomerang the gesture back to that person by paying him or her a compliment.

Now that we have considered ways to truly listen to what we are really saying – intentionally or unintentionally – whenever we communicate, the next secret will look at how to speak with mastery. In it, we will explore ways of saying what we want to say in the confidence that we will be understood.

Secret Five

Speak with Mastery

I f we want to communicate something and be understood, we have to do it in a way that makes sense to whoever is listening to us; it is a waste of time to do it any other way. That may sound ridiculously obvious, but think just how often you have not been fully understood: many times in your life, probably. The people whisperer takes full responsibility for being understood by other people. To help make this happen, the people whisperer delivers every message in such a way that it can be received easily and without confusion.

IDEAS FOR BEING UNDERSTOOD

There are many things we can do to assist ourselves in being understood, or – more accurately – we can help our listener to understand us. To be understood at all, we first have to have our listener's full attention. Although it is fairly obvious when someone's attention is elsewhere, we may need to be honest with ourselves when this is the case. We can experiment with getting people's attention in a variety of ways, some more socially acceptable than others: I find painting myself purple and dancing naked on top of the piano usually gets people's attention! If we want to hold the attention of someone with whom we are in a close relationship, we might simply ask that person to listen to us for a couple of minutes rather than competing with the TV, or putting more volume and edge in our voice (which will probably make our partner withdraw from us even further).

Sometimes it is better not to waste our energy. If we are quite simply not going to succeed in getting our listener's full attention, we might as well forget about communicating with them at that time, or in that set of circumstances, and save what we have to say for a more appropriate moment.

When we speak, we can make it as easy as possible for our listener by talking at a pace that allows them to think about what we are saying. Although we may be familiar with what we want to say, it could come as totally fresh information for the listener, who may need time to get their head around it. To that end, it's always best to use vocabulary, words and phrases that the listener knows. If someone is not 'getting it,' you can present your idea in different ways until you find the combination that unlocks it for the particular person you are talking to.

Always speak at a volume at which you can be heard! This is so important. If the listener has to strain to hear you because you are speaking too quietly, not only are you asking them to take on board your ideas, you are also making them have to work hard on your behalf in order to hear your ideas. If you have something worth while that you want to communicate, you need to deliver it at an audible volume, so that whoever you are talking to can see you believe in what you are saying and that you are not at all shy about it.

We are all quite sensitive creatures underneath our social, protective exteriors, so it is helpful to avoid presenting something in a way that questions or criticises the listener in any way whatsoever. An upset listener will shift their main focus from listening to what we're saying, and go on to defending them-selves. In effect, by upsetting them, we will have made them shut down and render them unable to hear us.

It is important to arrange our words before they come out of our mouth, rather than throw a load of words out into the air like a collection of obscure song lyrics, which we then try to arrange into something sensible. Make the communication count. Be precise and specific, and avoid being vague or making sweeping generalisations such as, 'I've seen millions of people do that sort of thing in countless different ways!' We might know what we mean, but someone receiving our ideas may have to do too much guesswork if what we say is not accurate or specific, and they may well not guess accurately, leading to misunderstandings, disagreements and finally all-out intercontinental war!

If we are asking someone for something, it is usually best to bite the bullet and ask for it straight. There is nothing to be gained from beating around the bush, suggesting what we want and hoping our listener will guess what we are after.

Take responsibility

Next time you talk to someone, take responsibility for getting that person to understand what you say. This can actually make mundane conversation very interesting – it becomes a little game to find the key to accessing each person's ability to hear you.

Speaking the Other's Language

One of the key skills for successful people whispering is the ability to communicate with anyone or anything you are with by speaking the language that they speak. Among the six billion or so people currently inhabiting the planet there are effectively six billion different languages being spoken, which means speaking a different language with every person you meet. Now that sounds like a challenging task! What we mean by this is not whether we speak French, German, English or Swahili. It is something more personal than that: speaking the other person's language helps them to feel recognised, comfortable and understood, and it can be done in a very subtle and loving way.

How does everyone create their own language?
We all have a totally unique set of experiences in our lives and ways of interpreting those experiences. This is why everyone develops their own way of communicating and why, in order to get the best from our relationships, it helps to speak other people's languages as much as we can.

Speaking another person's language does not mean that we have to give up our own beliefs or simply agree with their values and ideas. It simply means we accept their world-view as being the way they see things (however cock-eyed we might think it is!). It doesn't mean we can't disagree with anyone else.

How to speak the others' language

Honour how the person feels: Begin by being open to how someone feels inside. Allow your body to 'listen' to the energy levels of their body. Notice and accept whatever state they are in as being 'the state they are in': it will help you to relate to them more successfully. Remember that there is something very giving about making someone 'feel' at home in the communication you share with them.

Give people space: Ironically, one of the most effective ways to speak the other's language is to let them do more of the talking! As we saw in Secret Four, the more someone has a space where they feel they can safely express themselves, the more we are talking their language. We may think we have an important point to get across, but by allowing the other person to talk more, we can listen and learn their language. Then, when we do put our point across it will be so much more effective, because we will be speaking their language when we say it.

Ask people questions they want to answer: Another way to speak the other's language is to ask them questions with interest. This does not mean prying or demanding, just genuinely enquiring into their reality. You can actually work around to asking some very deep and personal questions by following this line of enquiry in a loving way. People are often moved when given the chance to speak about such things, and will share far more of themselves with us if we are speaking their language. This can make them quite vulnerable, and it also means we will have a responsibility to keep the things they say sacred and be trusted to safeguard the things that have been communicated to us.

Clean language: Using clean language has nothing to do with swearing. In fact, if the person you are talking to says *F**** this and *F**** that, it may help them to feel comfortable if you start *F-ing* along with them! Everyone has favourite words and phrases that they use and feel comfortable with, but the same word or phrase can mean different things to different people, e.g. the word 'food' can mean 'yummy' to one person, 'survival' to another and 'revulsion' to another. Clean language is about listening to the actual words other people use and then using exactly the same words or phrase that they just used . . . which leads us back again to the need to allow them to talk more, since we have to listen to hear what words and phrases they employ in order to use them ourselves.

Mirroring body posture and movements: People express a great deal about themselves and their inner feelings by the way they use their bodies. By and large, our bodies mirror how we feel. By moving in a similar way or taking up a similar posture to the other person, we can unconsciously make them feel that we understand them. We are essentially speaking their language with our bodies. What is interesting is how much we do this without even noticing. Next time you stand talking to someone; notice how they and you are standing and what you are both doing with your hands.

Touch, sight, sound: Everyone has preferences in the senses they prefer to use to experience life, and the words they use provide clues as to their preferred way. Using the same types of words and preferences as the other person in our communications with them will help us to connect with them much more effectively and lower any barriers between us. For example, some people prefer 'touch', so they might say, 'It *feels* like it is going to be a nice *warm* day'. Some people prefer sight, so they might say, 'It *looks* like its going to be a *bright* sunny day'. Some people prefer sound as their reference and they might say, 'I *hear* it is going to be sunny today: that will *ring* the changes'. (Very occasionally we may meet someone who is a 'taste' or 'smell' type of person, which can be really interesting. I will leave it up to you to play with possible options for words you might use!)

Using vocabulary that works

- Once you realise someone is a 'feeling' or 'touch' person, use words like warm, smooth, rough, hold, grip, grasp, handle, etc.
- Once you realise someone is a visual person, use words like light, dark, picture, vision, see, look, watch, red, blue, black and white, bright, etc.
- Once you realise someone is an audio person, use words like, ringing, heard, bang, sounds like, tell, voice, speak, hum, etc.

'Towards' and 'away from': Some people are more motivated by moving towards pleasant experiences; others are more motivated by moving away from unpleasant experiences. For example, 'towards' types might say, 'I love *going to the coast* on holiday and *getting into* the holiday mood'. An 'away-from' person might say, ' I love *stepping out* of the rat-race for a while, *getting away* from all the hassle by taking a holiday'.

Tone and speed: Notice the tone and speed of the other person's speech and try to match it. If you think about it, it is bound to be easier for you both to get along well if you are both talking in a similar way, rather than one of you speaking at the speed of light and all high-pitched, while the other one of you speaks sssssssslow and deep.

Being adaptable

As we have seen, speaking the other's language means being adaptable. It does not mean giving up who we are or flushing our own ideas away. It *does* mean temporarily adapting the way we frame things when talking to someone – in a loving way, not manipulatively, so that they understand us better than before. Speaking the other's language is not about betraying our own agenda or tricking the other person; it is about honouring their experience of life and who they really are. If we ever use these methods in a manipulative way, the other person's unconscious will sense it, since it is at that level that the deepest, most profound communication is actually taking place anyway.

Things to do:

1. Whilst remaining true to yourself inside, suspend your own opinions and ideas for a while and experiment with your conversations. Speaking the other's language is a bit like canoeing across a fast-flowing river. To get to the other side you first need to go with the flow of the river, then gradually guide the canoe over to where you want to be. First enter the stream of someone else's flow by speaking their language, then guide the communication to where you want it to go. Lovingly, of course.
2. Listen with objective interest, not just to *what* people are saying, but *how* they are saying it.

Mixed Messages

Giving clear and succinct messages and directions is essential if we wish to be understood. People whisperers know that this means avoiding mixed messages by communicating with absolute focus and clarity. Mixed messages communicate more than one conflicting idea at the same time, on a verbal, physical, emotional or energy level. They leave us not quite knowing what to do, what the communicator meant or which message to listen to. Mixed messages are everywhere and they can make otherwise ordinary communication give rise to all kinds of difficulties and misunderstandings.

Mixed messages can slow down or hinder relationships between people. Someone receiving mixed messages has to spend more time figuring out exactly what was meant. They may also be unable to act because they don't know which message to follow and this can lead to a lack of trust. When we express ourselves without mixed messages, we bring clarity and understanding to our relationships and help people to know where they stand.

When we give out mixed messages, we not only confuse the other person, we also make ourselves appear weaker, because what we are saying is not direct, clear and focused, but spread out and diluted. Mixed messages make us sound unsure of ourselves and diminish our personal power. Eventually people may even begin to ignore us because they have been confused too many times already. Regularly giving out mixed messages is a bit like crying 'wolf'.

Types of mixed messages

Sometimes we think we are communicating something to someone, but it doesn't come across the way we think it does. This is because each one of us has our own language, so while we may be expressing something in the way that *we* understand, it may sound completely different to our listener. This can confuse the listener and even make the listener feel uptight. Although that person is listening to us say something, what is being said doesn't quite resonate or ring true – which is probably quite right, because your listener is not really getting what you originally meant to say. To avoid this happening, we can speak the other person's language, put ourselves in the listener's shoes, hear the message through their ears and find a way that they can understand to get our original meaning across.

Focus and vision

Sometimes we may say something but don't have a true belief in it or clear vision about what we are saying ourselves. Our communication will be much stronger if we say the same thing with voice, body and soul than if our beliefs or vision do not match our words. We can see this in politician's eyes quite often and hear it in the 'voice' behind their speaking voice when they try to convince us of something, but they don't hold that truth in themselves. An example might be when a president says, 'I did not have sexual relations with that woman (cough, splutter) . . .'

There may be times when we intentionally avoid being straight down the line in what we say and 'fuzzy up' the picture by using mixed messages. That way, we cannot be pinned down as to what exactly we mean. Then, if what we have to say is not received favourably we can use the mixed meanings of our message to construct a maze or camouflage so as to protect ourselves against ridicule, attack or perceived failure. None of us like our beliefs, our opinions or ourselves to be judged as wrong or lacking, so presenting mixed messages can 'save' us from being shot down, but ultimately they may lead to even greater confusion and cause us more trouble than they are worth.

Things to do:

1. Listen to the way people speak to each other, especially when making requests. See how they often avoid saying something totally openly and directly.
2. Look into your own heart and speak honestly, openly and totally clearly. Ask for what you want: keep it plain and simple.
3. Separate your communications with gaps, so that you won't run one message into another and mix them up.
4. Check that you are being 'congruent' – that means that your words, body, heart and mind are sending the same message. If someone does not understand you, check that you are giving a plain, unmixed message.

YOUR TRUE VOICE

As we have seen, the actual words we choose create the kind of experiences, communication and relationships we experience. However, it is not only our words that carry power, but also the way in which we use our voice and the way in which we speak. The people whisperer always speaks with their 'true voice', from a place of respect, integrity, resonance and heart. The people whisperer listens with attention and insight when people speak and is aware of which part of themselves they speak from; consequently, the people whisperer hears whether it is their true voice with which they speak.

Your Voice is Totally Unique

Question

Your voice is a very public expression of who you are. Your voice is also an expression of *how* you are: it lets people know how you are feeling inside. Ask yourself: how does your mood affect your voice and how does your voice affect your mood?

Whatever it sounds like, the voice is a beautiful instrument with which we interact with other people, not only through our choice of words, but through the tone, pitch, speed and emotion with which the sound comes out of our mouth. Moreover, our voice will sound differently and communicate different messages depending on where we speak from inside ourselves. Our voice lets people know whether we speak from a place of integrity, insecurity, conviction, truth, untruth, love, bewilderment, confusion, confidence, clarity, insincerity, commitment, strength, tenderness, intimacy or one of many other places within.

It is useful to realise that the way our voice sounds to the outside world is entirely different to the way it sounds in our head. Have you ever wondered what your voice sounds like to the outside world? Have you ever recorded your voice or heard it played back? What was your reaction? Quite likely it was something like 'Oh no, is that my voice? That's not what I sound like is it?' People who hear our voice all of the time don't react like that when we speak, do they? Well, hopefully not! Take the time to listen to the sound of your voice: to notice what its tone, pitch and resonance are like.

People we know well have voices that are instantly recognisable to us: that means in less than a quarter of a second we know who they are and mostly what mood they are in or how they feel.

Ask yourself:

◆ Who feels soothed or loved by the sound of your voice?
◆ Who jumps up or feels anxious when you raise your voice?
◆ Whom can you move with your voice?
◆ Who ignores your voice?
◆ Who overpowers your voice with their own voice?
◆ What effect might being told to 'keep quiet' have had on you in your formative years?

◆ How much do you open your mouth and allow your true voice to come out?

◆ Ask yourself, 'What might I be hiding or keeping from the world by not fully opening my mouth and expressing my message?'

Resonance: Resonance is the breadth, richness and 'ring' to the sound. People who speak with resonance are allowing the sound to be created within their whole self, like a clear bell. They do not restrict, dampen or pinch the sound; they allow it to ring through their being, so that it is a pleasure to listen to.

Opening your mouth: It can feel strange to open your mouth even a fraction more than you are used to, but it can make such a difference to how much of your voice is 'allowed' out. You may have a voice that could inspire people to greatness, but if it is trapped inside your mouth, the only things to hear the inspiration are your teeth, tongue and tonsils and, although they have their uses, much of your inspirational voice will be wasted on them!

The power in your voice: The power in your voice is *NOT ABOUT THE VOLUME!* It is about where your voice comes from and how much conviction and presence you put into the way you speak. It is also about how much belief, value and importance you place in what you have to say and how much commitment you have to communicating it. Power in the voice is not something to use to force our way into a conversation or overpower someone else's voice; power is something that is very incisive and compelling, so that when we do speak, people listen and hear what we have to say.

Breath – supporting your voice: Your voice is like the tip of the iceberg: it is the part that is in evidence to the outside world, but there is much going on under the surface to support your message. It is the way you use your breath to support your voice that gives the voice its ability to speak from a solid base.

◆ Use your breath to expand your voice, to fill the sails of your words.

◆ Give yourself time and permission to take in the air you need before you speak, so that your voice is held on a cushion of air and therefore sounds lighter, more solid and more comfortable.

◆ Notice where the air needs to go to and come from in your body. Explore opening your ribs when you take air in; not just the front of the ribs, but the sides, under your armpits and the back of your ribs.

Speaking with Your Whole Body

Speaking from the heart: When we speak from the heart, our voice carries a message of passion, conviction, belief, truth, compassion and love. When someone is speaking from the heart it can be very moving to the listener. To speak from the heart, focus on your heart and chest, allow the feelings you associate with this part of you come out of your chest, open your heart and trust that it is safe to speak with openness and resonance from this part of you.

Speaking from the head: When someone speaks from the head, they are often analysing, intellectualising, rationalising and expressing thought processes. Speaking from this place is very useful in certain circumstances, as it can help people to understand the mechanics of what is happening and to see their way around problems in a practical way. But there is a danger that we may lose touch with our feelings, and consequently those around us if we speak too much from the head.

Speaking from the stomach/centre: This area of the body is the power centre. When we speak from here we speak with conviction and centredness. A voice that comes from this place has a sense of strength, security and belief behind it. Have you ever noticed times when you speak from this place in your body? How is it for you to do that? What effect does it have on those around you? If you don't know how to speak from your power centre, think about a subject you feel absolutely clear and strongly about and put your attention on your stomach while you speak. You may be surprised by the power that you can produce in speaking this way.

Speaking from the face and nose: Our face is the main part of us through which we show our expressions to the world. When your voice is speaking your message, do you also express the same message with your face? The bones around our cheeks, nose and eyes are a major source of resonance to our voice. If we hold our face in a tight or pinched way, especially the nose, it restricts the ability of the voice to express our true message.

Speaking from the throat: The throat is a very important channel through which our voice comes up from our body and out into the world. If we speak only from our throat, we will restrict the ability of our voice to come from a deeper place. To speak from the throat and allow it to sound whole, the throat and neck need to be open and relaxed. If we are tense, the first place to tighten is often the throat and neck. What then follows is a voice that is tight and thin, with a limited palette for expression. Think how difficult it would be to speak clearly if someone had hold of us around the throat, yet we often do that to ourselves internally through fear or tension.

Projecting your voice to where you want it to go

It is far more effective to send your voice out into the world if you know where you want it to go – if you have a clear idea of where you want it to go or who you want to 'get it'. Often we talk and let the words fall out of our mouths and disperse into the ether, but if we believe we are speaking our truth with the intention of being heard, we need to be aware of the direction and distance we want our voice to travel. If we were firing a water pistol at someone, we would aim it in their direction and with a trajectory that would make it go the right distance. The same simple action works for the voice.

Speed and pitch

Our voice changes its speed and pitch depending on the people or situation in which we find ourselves. When you are in a comfortable situation with company that respects and listens to your voice, what is the speed and pitch like? How is it different when you are uncomfortable?

Volume

Are you skipping this bit because it is quieter than all the rest? Hopefully not. Sometimes it helps to project the voice: and volume plays a part in that. Sometimes too much volume makes people switch off – their ears take too much battering and they quit listening. Sometimes we need enough volume to reach someone who is a little further away. However, volume alone doesn't get a message across over distances; simplifying the message and speaking at a speed and in a language that the listener can understand will also help.

True volume in the voice comes from a combination of speaking from the right place in the body, resonance and support with the breath. When projecting your voice, allow the volume to come from inside you. Give it space and avoid any sense of pushing or trying to be loud, as this will most likely bring tension into the voice and your true voice will not be heard.

Tuning into Other People's Voices

Now that we have looked in some detail at how our voices represent us and reflect our inner state, it is interesting to notice how other people's voices represent them to the outside world. We can note what messages they are conveying and whether these are the same as the messages they are *trying* to convey.

◆ Does the way other people speak make you feel inspired, bored, strained, excited or interested?
◆ Do they speak slowly, quickly, with resonance or thinly, high pitched or low?
◆ How does the way they speak affect your ability and willingness to give them your attention and receive their message?

When listening to others, it can also be interesting to see if you can tell where they are speaking from – the head, the heart, the body, the forked tongue or whether they are speaking for someone who is not even present.

Things to do:

1. Listen to the sound of your voice while you speak to different people in different situations, such as in the shops, on the phone, at the bank, at work or round the dining room table. When and where does it sound most effective, inviting, secure, inspiring, interesting, clear and communicative?
2. Record yourself speaking. Do this until you feel entirely comfortable listening to your voice!
3. When you are listening to other people speaking, 'open' yourself, so that you are truly listening and can feel whereabouts in their body they are speaking from: the heart, the throat, the head, the forked tongue etc.
4. Practise speaking and directing the sound in a specific direction and at a specific speed towards its destination. Listen to the route the sound takes from your mouth, over to where you wish it to go.
5. When you speak, notice which parts of your face and body resonate or vibrate subtly with the sound. See how releasing or relaxing parts of your body can make your voice seem more full, resonant and powerful.
6. See how different your speech is if you consciously take in just the right amount of air before you begin. Before speaking, experiment with 'breathing' the air into different parts of your body by imagining drawing the breath right down into the relevant area. Note how this can change your voice.

Having looked at the ways in which we communicate verbally, and what it means to use our true voice, in the next Secret we will consider what happens when we meet people and how to enjoy fulfilling relationships.

Secret Six:

Enjoy Fulfilling Relationships

THE VALUE OF MEETING

Meeting people plays a large part in how we create opportunities for happiness, love, prosperity and success in our lives. The quality of those meetings dictates the level of possibility for happiness, love, prosperity and success. This is why skilful people whisperers appreciate the joys and benefits of meeting people: thriving on interaction and the sense of possibility that it creates, and endeavouring to bring presence and value to every meeting and every person we meet.

The best kind of meeting is one in which everyone feels comfortable to be in each other's presence, and in which everyone has the opportunity to manifest gifts in some way. It stands to reason that someone who is 'well met' will be more inclined to give us whatever they can than someone who is 'ill met'. Helping other people to feel comfortable when we meet them is undoubtedly the best way forward, for us as well as for them. Even if they don't give as much we do, we will still have benefited. And if we allow them to take too much from us or to make us feel uncomfortable, they will have lost, because we may just avoid them in future.

First Impressions

Ask yourself:

◆ What kind of impression do you make when you first meet someone?

◆ What judgements, assessments and assumptions do you make about others from first impressions?

If we hold any kinds of judgements, assumptions, preconceived or fixed ideas about the meeting or whom we encounter in it, we erect a barrier to the flow of possibilities that may arise from it. Even if we have met someone before, we cannot be sure that that person will behave in the same way when we next meet them. They may have stuff going on in their lives that we cannot see or know about that drives their behaviour, and whatever drove their behaviour the last time we met them may not be doing so on the next occasion.

As well as not judging those whom we meet, we can think about what impression our presence and body language gives to people when we first meet them. Creating the best impression we can does not mean that we have to pretend to be someone or something we are not. In fact, the way to give the best impression of ourselves is to be true to our selves, whilst being aware of the other person's presence too.

When we meet anyone, their body language will also tell us a lot about them. It is worth checking to see if it matches their words. Are they putting up barriers because they are defensive or feel insecure? It is surprising how many people are insecure, nervous or have background fear when we meet them. Their fear may not be generated by us, but from some faulty software that was unwittingly installed in their minds in the past.

Ways to Create Positive Meetings

Create space: To create positive meetings with anyone in any situation, give the person or people you meet room in which to be themselves. Ask questions that help you to understand them and that allow them to enjoy sharing things about themselves with you.

Check your body's response: From time to time, check your body internally: you want to feel peaceful and calm inside. (See Secret Three: Trust Your Body.) Feel your body 'open' up to the other person, so that you are sending out friendly energy alongside your verbal conversation. Remember that your external body also needs attention. Check what conversation your body is having with the other person's body, so that you are sure your body is saying what you want it to say! As you pay attention to what your body is outwardly saying, attempt to make it appear passive and relaxed, as that is what works best in most situations. Have your eyes looking soft and present. Look at the other person, but not in a staring or threatening way.

Handshakes: It is not so usual these days to shake hands during informal encounters in the Western world. Nevertheless, handshakes can be very interesting as there are so many things that they can tell you about someone. A weedy handshake like a lettuce leaf might be saying 'I'm timid', 'I'm not really here' or 'I'm not really interested in you'. A strong handshake can be a way of trying to dominate, as if saying, 'Aren't I strong and tough; look, I can hurt your hand, even though my mouth is smiling'. A very brief handshake might be saying, 'I haven't got much time for you'. A handshake where a finger secretly tickles your palm can mean either, 'I'll meet you around the back of the bike sheds' or 'Are you also a member of an ancient, secret, male-only society?' . . .

Preparing for Difficult Meetings

Sometimes we may suspect that a meeting is going to be difficult but we have to go ahead with it anyway, whether it is with our partner or spouse, the bank manager, a job interviewer, a blind date, our boss or our children's head teacher! There are ways we can prepare for these encounters that will help us to stay balanced in them and prevent energy being taken from us.

Pay attention to your emotions as soon as they start to become unsettled, which may be just before you knock on the door or it may be a day, a week or months before! However long before the meeting it is when your emotions start to stir themselves up, practise allowing them to subside. Remember that stilling your emotions will be easier when they are only slightly rippling rather than when they are fully formed tidal waves. Being able to still your emotions will help you to avoid reacting or saying something inappropriate or impulsive in the meeting.

Before we go into a meeting, we can visualise having an invisible shield or defensive bubble around us in order to protect ourselves from any hateful or harmful attack. Although this may sound whacky, it really works, and there is no particular way that it has to be done. Experiment and find a way that works for you personally.

We can also use our physical body to still our emotions, which in turn will help still our mind. By keeping our attention focused on our lower stomach, we can help ourselves to stay centred and grounded. It can help to think of our feet as roots that anchor us down into earth, and to feel *both* of our feet in contact with the ground. Simply being still, sitting or standing in a way that is comfortable for us, so that we can be physically quiet during the meeting, will communicate personal power to other people as well to ourselves. Fiddling about or constantly adjusting the body are obvious signs of discomfort.

In a difficult meeting, remember to allow the other person or people to do most of the talking: 'a closed mouth gathers no feet!' Gather as few feet as possible by letting others express their stuff as much as you can. When you do speak, say exactly what you mean in a way that they will understand. Avoid speaking hurriedly. Listen to your tone of voice. Breathe in enough air before talking. Use phrases such as:

'I accept that is how it is for you.'

'I guess we could agree to disagree.'

'You have a point there: maybe you're right.'

'This is how it is for me.'

'I am sorry that you feel that way.'

Things to do:

1. Enjoy all of your interactions and meetings with people. See every meeting as being filled with potential: you never know who or where the next incredible phase of your life will come from or from whom.

Aim to leave everyone you meet happier than they were before you arrived.

2. Explore what happens for you emotionally, mentally and physically when you are with different people.

3. Remind yourself that most other people are at least as insecure in company as you, even if they don't know that they are or they appear to be the opposite.

4. Treat everyone in a way in which you would like to be treated by them.

BEING COMFORTABLE WITH STRANGERS

We have seen how the way we are when we meet people can profoundly influence our potential experiences and relationships in life. Now let's explore using communication skills in the company of strangers.

Strangers present previously untapped possibilities for us, and it is often through our meetings with strangers that our lives are taken into new and exciting phases. We, in turn, could be offering untapped possibilities for their lives, too. What happens when we put together two chemicals that have never been introduced before? Well, who knows – anything is possible! OK, so there could be a cataclysmic explosion, but equally there could be a discovery that sets humanity free from some of the bonds that tie them. Being with people we have never met before may offer all manner of potential gifts; all we need to do is be there, stay open and nurture the situation. However comfortable or uncomfortable we may feel when we meet strangers, it is worth remembering that underneath, all people are human beings, and underneath that, we are all part of the same life force.

Ask yourself:

◆ When you meet strangers, do you ever feel uncomfortable or wonder what they think of you?

◆ Have you ever thought that they may be feeling uncomfortable and wondering what you think of them?

◆ Can you let go of your thinking, judging and forming of opinions about another person completely when you first meet them, and how might that change the uncomfortable feelings you have?

When we don't know someone, it can be easy for us to imagine that they are more accomplished in life, more successful, more intelligent, more powerful or generally more important than we are. But everyone comes into this world via the same basic route: a sperm and an egg get together, the baby grows in the womb and is born. The baby is helpless, cries, eats, cries, eats, vomits and fills nappies, grows up, lives however many years are allotted and then departs this world when the body gives out. This is the same for everyone. Once we can be with strangers and recognise that they are equal beings, we can take that invisible bond of equality that we share one step further: we can meet them with love, knowing that we are all a part of the same life force, part of the same creation, that they are us and we are them.

However, when we meet someone for the first time, there is often a part of us that automatically forms opinions, ideas and judgements about them, and we may even habitually form these opinions before we are actually face to face with them. By dropping our assessments of someone else, we begin a process of dropping our concerns about what they might think of us. It is an odd truth, but letting go of critical thoughts about strangers will actually make us feel more comfortable with them and more comfortable within ourselves.

If we give strangers the space to be who they really are, they will unconsciously begin to accept the space from us as a gift. And, as they enter the space we have given them, we will begin to feel more comfortable ourselves, as we will no longer be the victim of our own preconceptions, fears or reservations.

Preparing to Meet Strangers

When we have to meet strangers, we can prepare ourselves to meet them by first being aware of our breath going in and out of our body. By focusing on it, we allow it to bring any anxiety to rest, much as the stirred up mud in a pond will gradually sink to the bottom if it is allowed to.

The more we focus on maintaining a calm inner state and keeping our attention on the 'space', the more flow we will bring to our meeting with strangers, so we don't feel we have to rush in and impress or take control of the situation. We can allow some space into the room by making conversation at a measured pace, and ask interested questions and listen with interest to the answers they give. We don't have to be the life and soul of a situation to bring value to it.

What do you talk about or say when you meet strangers?
To find out what to talk about, we can ask questions and give the other person space in which to talk and express who they are. In other words, it means speaking the other's language. By asking questions and finding out what makes the other person tick, we can discover what common ground we have, or at least what ground they feel comfortable talking about. This is important, as finding common ground puts other people at their ease and, if we can do that, we will have more space in which to be ourselves as well.

If you ever experience uncomfortable silences when you are with a stranger, instead of trying to fill the silence by talking, focus your attention on your 'inner space', and let the silence 'be'. The company of strangers will no longer feel so uncomfortable. In a sense you could ask yourself, do we really need to talk that much, anyway?

Remember that we are all equals. During our lifetime we all have different experiences – different parents, circumstances, good habits, bad habits, virtues, talents, good fortune and bad. But the bottom line is that we are all equal beings: you, me, the Queen, the Pope, your local bus driver, the kids on your street corner, the chief executive of the company you work for etc ... At the end of the day, we are all equal.

Shyness

Shyness is universally common, so once we realise that most people *feel* shy in some situations, it may not seem such a disadvantage to us. The truth is that what we focus on grows; so if we are feeling shy in certain company and start focusing on our shyness – which is what we usually do – it will increase! Instead of focusing on our shyness, it helps to focus on something else, such as the other person or people. If we let go of the need to prove ourselves and stop thinking we *should* be a certain way, but just relax and be who we are, self-contained and peaceful inside, the shyness will fade away. Remember that some of the people who appear least shy are often the most shy. During my previous work as a musician and performer, I realised that one of the ways people cope with major shyness and insecurity is to hide it by becoming performers, thereby coming across as the total opposite of shy.

Things to do:

1. Next time you are going into a situation with strangers, remember that they may feel as insecure as you do. Approach things as though that is the case and see what happens if you take steps to make them feel more at ease. Focus on the inner state of your body: simply be aware of what it is doing. This can have miraculous effects.

2. Practise being totally yourself in situations with people with whom you feel comfortable. That means not pretending to be anything that you are not. Take the comfortable feeling you have and bring it into meetings with strangers.

3. Give strangers the room to express themselves: encourage them to speak about themselves and what interests them. The more interesting you find them, the better it is for you.

4. Look for ways to meet more and more strangers: they are part of the stream that brings newness into your life and will take you on to the next stage of your life.

5. Deliberately seek out situations in which you feel slightly shy, such as when meeting new people or public speaking. Gradually build up from small occasions such as informal gatherings in the pub to larger events, such as speaking at weddings or office meetings. Keep working on overcoming your feelings of shyness and becoming more comfortable in a challenging situation.

CREATING RAPPORT

'Rapport' is the knack of creating a connection between ourselves and someone else that enables us to share common ground and travel together in some way, be it in a conversation, through working together, loving each other, raising a family or creating some great works. Being good at creating rapport means knowing how to get on with people: empathising, identifying, being authentic and honest, being happy about who we are and not judging who they are. Rapport is a catalyst towards co-operation. Rapport skills are a key tool for people whisperers, because of the value of finding common ground with people and understanding the possibilities that are created as a result of having good rapport.

The Benefits of Creating Rapport

When we are in rapport with someone, everything we do with that person will go more smoothly. We will be more in the flow and, metaphorically speaking, able to go further on the same amount of fuel. Although true rapport is something that cannot be forced, theoretically it's possible to create rapport with anyone. That said, sometimes we may come across people who are resistant to rapport with us; if so, we will have to decide at which point we want to stop investing energy in the relationship and accept that we have done all that we can do there, for now.

How to create rapport

To help people develop rapport with us, we have to be true to our selves as much as is possible or appropriate. If we are not our true selves, it can be quite difficult for anyone to develop rapport with us, as they won't know which of our 'selves' to connect with.

In conversations, we may find it best to use the word 'yes' more than the word 'no'. An appropriate level of humour can also be helpful to loosen things up, but we will need to be careful not to use humour at the expense of others, even someone who is not around. If we joke about someone not present, the person we're with could well be right to assume we might joke about them when they are not around. It is best to avoid any attempts to come across as bigger, better or more impressive than we really are, or to dominate the conversation. These sorts of behaviour tend to push people away and take up too much space; they do not create rapport; they generally snuff it out.

Things to do:

1. When you are with someone, even on first meeting, in what ways do you behave, speak or express yourself that may affect the other person?

2. Make a list of the people with whom you have good rapport. What are the benefits in your relationship of your rapport with each person? Now, think of some of the possible benefits that might come out of creating more rapport with people with whom you only have an acquaintance at present.

3. Watch the way people interact with each other and notice how they build or destroy rapport by the way they are. Think of some people who are good at creating rapport. How do they do it? What types of behaviours make you feel comfortable with them; make you feel you could wear the same team shirts, that you share common views; that you could work well or that you could create something worth while together?

LOVE AND APPROVAL

Expressing love and approval are probably two of the greatest ways you can connect with others known to man or beast. The people whisperer knows that we all thrive when we receive love and approval, and understands what wonderful and helpful gifts these qualities are to exchange with others, as well as to give to one's self.

What We Do for Love

Everything we do in life is motivated by something that makes us get up and make the effort. Much of our day-to-day routine might be about looking after our basic human needs for survival such as food, shelter, etc., but, at a deeper level, a lot of our interaction with other people is about our wanting to be loved. Working to receive love and approval is mostly done unconsciously, but is a very powerful motivator in our lives. Love that is unconditional, dependable and undemanding, like the love of a good parent, gives us a strong base on which to build and live our lives.

Love and approval begin with YOU
Many of us are raised to put 'others first and ourselves second' or told 'it is better to give than to receive', but whilst these phrases may be very charitable, unless we ourselves know how to receive, we may not fully understand how to give to someone else with balance and in a way in which they can also receive. Many of us may find giving easier than receiving, as being be able to receive without resistance requires us to believe we are deserving and 'good enough'.

Ask yourself:

◆ How much do you love and appreciate yourself? Do you love and appreciate yourself less than the other people in your life? Do you think you are unworthy of being loved and appreciated? Do you feel uncomfortable with the idea of loving yourself?
◆ How often do you compliment yourself on something done well? How do you feel when you or someone else compliments you on something done well?
◆ How do you respond when someone shows you love and approval: by showing thanks and giving love to them in return, or by feeling awkward and rejecting their gift?

Giving love and approval
Giving love doesn't mean going up to the people in our lives and gushing all over them, although that may be well received in certain company: people have different capacities for receiving love and approval, and the people whisperer will be sensitive to delivering these gifts in ways that they all can receive. One person may need us to be a little more tactile, another may need us to be

less tactile; one may need us to express love in more open ways and yet another may need us to give love so subtly that it is nothing but a thought sent out on the ether.

If someone has received our love and approval, something between us and them will have changed. Things will *seem* different. They may be more comfortable within themselves and start reaching out to us. Often someone to whom we have given love and approval will want to give back to us spontaneously.

Sometimes we may not be able to tell if our love has been received, but if we know we have given in a way that they could receive, then that is our part in the process. Sometimes we simply have to put love out there to someone, stand back, give them space and let go of wanting any particular outcome.

What someone else does or doesn't do with the love we give, or shows or doesn't show outwardly, is up to them. We are being even more loving to them by allowing them the freedom to respond to our gift in whatever way they wish and in a way that is right for them . . . if they appear to respond at all, that is.

Approval is more than just saying 'Thanks for doing that job' or 'Thanks for passing that coffee'; it is a way of saying 'Thanks for being who you are' and 'Thanks for sharing this time and energy with me'. Showing approval to someone when they have reached out to us lets them know that we have recognised the energy they have given to us. But showing too much approval, disproportionate to what they have done for us, may weaken our position because it tells the other person that we are hungry for their energy and are in danger of wanting to feed off them.

Resistance to Being Loved and Appreciated

Paradoxically, although one of the most powerful motivators in people's lives is the wish to be loved and appreciated, it is very common for us to resist receiving love and approval. Sometimes we make it hard for people to give us love, praise or thanks, as though we are not worthy of these things. We may attach fear to feeling loved and appreciated, perhaps as though, if we were to allow another person to help us feel these things, they would gain some kind of ownership over us and be in a position to control, hurt or let us down. This is something to bear in mind whenever someone does not appear to be receiving the love and approval that we have been giving them: their resistance to receiving love and approval might stem from a fear of being vulnerable.

It is easy to think that incredibly self-confident people or those who are in positions of power, such as people in high positions in corporations, don't need these gifts of love and approval, but inside they are still human. In fact, leaders and people at the top can find it hard to meet their need for love and approval, since their position means they have to appear so 'together' and watertight. Sometimes, people at the top are only there because they were driven by an unbalanced and over-needy desire to be loved and approved of. Think about it: most of us would be happy to be shown love and approval by a dozen or so people in our lives, but a politician wants the whole population to vote for him or her and give their approval . . . now that *is* needy!

The Dance of Giving and Receiving

Once we realise that the wish for love and approval is a universal motivator, we can begin to dance with the flow of love by helping others to meet that need through their connections with us. And as we help others to meet those needs by being with us, the positive flow of giving Love comes back to us.

It is not healthy to give love and approval with the intention of doing it solely to receive something back from the other person: that would change it from giving into manipulating . . . the dance would become a series of contrived, wooden steps (a bit like me trying to Salsa, actually!).

The gifts we receive in return for giving love and approval are an incidental result of the process, not the reason to do it in the first place.

◆ *Remember* that Universal law always brings back to you what you have given out, so a return gift of love might come from an unexpected source or in a way that you don't expect.
◆ *Remember* that giving love and approval is an on-going job, not something to do once or twice and then quit, justifying

yourself by thinking 'Oh, they already know I love and appreciate them'.

Acceptance is Pure Love

One of the purest ways to give love and approval is to accept someone exactly as they are, with all of their foibles, traits, 'faults', habits and ways of being. This is incredibly liberating for people, because once we accept someone totally as they are, they will unconsciously know that they are loved, as we see past the behaviour to the pure 'being' underneath. This opens a whole realm of possibilities, some of which people may find quite emotionally charged, as many of us have never been accepted exactly and totally as we are. We are used to the feeling of not being quite right or good enough or truly loved for ourselves, so the state of *not* being fully accepted actually feels more familiar and safe. Once we do feel totally fine as we are ... well! That can be scary – that means we are good enough, more than good enough, we are wonderful and lovable.

Ask yourself:

◆ How do the people in your life show you that you are loved?
◆ In what ways would you like them to show you love and approval?
◆ Have you asked them to show you love and approval in a way that they can understand?
◆ How do you show the people in your life that they are loved?
◆ Have you asked them what makes them feel loved by you?

Things to do:

1. What are your five best attributes? Write them down. Now think of five more! Write them down. Now think of five more! Write them down – yes, really do it. Now think of five more! Write them down. Yes, really, *really* do it! Identify any resistance you might have to feeling comfortable about receiving love and approval, either from yourself or from others, and look for opportunities to give love and approval to yourself.

2. Explore ways to give love and approval to at least five people in your life. Include your friends, your family and work colleagues. The ways you show your love and approval can be subtle or more obvious, depending on what is appropriate for each person. You might greet a colleague warmly in the corridor, buy your partner a huge bunch of roses, or send a message of love and appreciation to someone through your thoughts or from your heart.

EXCHANGING ENERGY

We have looked at some of the more obvious ways in which people whisperers communicate, such as through words, the voice, creating rapport and body talk. Now let's move on to something that may be less apparent but which is very exciting and which is everywhere in every moment: energy.

Energy flows in a huge number of ways between us and the other people in our world. It is exchanged in the words we use, in the emotions and intentions behind our words and actions, in our actions themselves, through giving and receiving money, through being in another's space and through sex (oh yes!). Science seems to be proving that everything in the universe is essentially pure energy: the stars, the planets, solid objects, thin air, you, me, everyone else and our emotions included. In fact, because everything in the Universe is energy, there is just no getting away from it so we may as well flow with it.

There are many different kinds of energy: energy that is explosive; energy that is creative; energy that is peaceful, loving and comforting; energy that restores and repairs; energy that gets things done; energy that can only sustain short bursts; energy that is steady and long-lasting; energy that is playful; energy that is heavy and serious; energy that is light and uplifting; energy that is quietly secure; energy that is searching and unsettled . . . There are endless types of energy, but all basically emanating from the same raw material.

Any time we are with other people there is a flow of energy going on. Even when we are not actually in someone's vicinity, energy can still be flowing between ourselves and them. Sometimes there is a real surge of energy, sometimes a trickle. Sometimes the energy is mostly one-way, from one person to the other. Sometimes the flow of energy back and forth between people is more evenly balanced. Sometimes this flow of energy is healthy and sometimes it isn't.

Successful people whisperers are always aware of the flow of energy between people and manage their own energy levels accordingly, enjoying healthy exchanges of energy. They realise that it is essential to be vigilant during unhealthy exchanges of energy and take steps to protect themselves. Remember, as we saw in Secret Two, we do not have to be talking to someone or within earshot of them to be communicating: we will still be communicating on an energy level, whether we are audible or not.

What is 'energy'?

The concept of energy may sound a little bit vague and fluffy, but actually it is very real. Let me direct you towards some examples . . . Do you have certain people in your life who leave you feeling drained and tired after you've been with them? Do you have other people in your life who leave you feeling buzzing, high or inspired? We all know certain individuals who make us feel either drained or energised, and, if possible, we could all do with spending more time with the latter and less time with the former.

Managing Energy

Before we start to become responsible for the exchange of energy between ourselves and other people, it is a good idea to become aware of, and responsible for, our own levels of energy. Of course our energy levels go up and down at various times according to our bio-rhythms and whatever is going on around us. If we are involved in a dull task (sitting in boring school lessons comes to mind) our energy levels are liable to be down; if we are doing something exciting (like being out on an eagerly anticipated first date) our energy levels will be up.

Aside from that, each of us tends to have energy levels that are characteristic of our personalities, which is fine provided that these levels do not cause difficulties when we interact with other people. For example, a highly energetic person might sometimes be 'too much' for a quieter friend, which would not help the two to communicate. Equally, a low-energy person who is trying to get a point across to someone with high energy levels might wish to increase their own energy levels in order to match their hyper companion. To manage our own energy levels in many situations is quite simple: guess what we need to do first . . . yes, be 'aware' of our energy levels. Becoming aware of our personal energy levels is simply a matter of taking the time to notice what is happening in us.

◆ **Ask yourself:** What is my energy level like at the moment? For example, is it low, near death, high or explosively hyper?
◆ **Next, ask yourself:** In this situation, what would be the most beneficial energy level?
◆ **Then ask:** Is my current level of energy an appropriate match for talking to this person? If it is, great! If it is too high, 'allow' the energy in your body and mind to lower; if it is too low, take in some energy-giving breath, think exciting thoughts and raise your levels.

Healthy energy

Healthy exchanges of energy happen between people when no one involved feels depleted as a result of their being together; even better, the participants all feel that they have been energised by the meeting. In order for a healthy exchange of energies to take place each person is required to accept the other(s), to validate their views and to give them respect and the space in which to be themselves. That doesn't mean you can't disagree, but ideally any disagreement will not carry a negative emotional charge with it, whereby the winner draws energy from the loser and the loser suffers a loss of energy. (We will look at this in more detail in Secret Ten.)

We get back whatever we give out, so if we can intentionally help others to gain energy from being with us, without it costing or depleting us, we will receive all manner of benefits in return.

Let's say you are in business and every client you talk to or see feels lifted by meeting you. Your clients will probably want to see more of you and buy more of your products, buy you lunch, tell other people about you, give you energy in return and may even try to headhunt you and offer you a more rewarding job with twice the money! On the other hand, if you drain precious energy from your business clients, they will attempt to see you as little as possible. They will feel exhausted when they talk to you; probably try to restrict any amount of energy they send your way in the form of money and they may tell other people what a drag you are or at the very least not mention you at all.

If you help your loving partner feel a positive flow of energy, they will feel inclined to spend more time interacting with you rather than watching TV, being out with their mates or staying late at work. They will look forward to being with you, talking to you, being close and exchanging energies with you in many ways, not least making love and sharing tenderness and intimacy. If you deplete energy from your partner what might they do? Well, you may know that already . . . Think about ways to bring positive energy flows to both personal and business relationships.

Unhealthy energy

It is fine to exchange, give and receive energy with another person if we agree to it, but it is not fine if that person begins to take energy from us without our 'permission'. In an unhealthy exchange of energy, one person endeavours, often unconsciously, to gain energy by affecting the emotional state of the other – perhaps by making them feel bad, frustrated, angry, confused, belittled, controlled or by dominating the situation using overt aggression or subversive, sneaky ways. By trying to make themselves look better than us or have a more valid and superior opinion, someone can draw energy off us and use it to build up their own energy level.

Often, someone will draw energy off another by using their intimate knowledge of that person's vulnerable areas. This is why it can sometimes be risky to get very close to another person: unless they are very delicate with us, they can easily draw energy off us by using that closeness to get under our armour. Have you ever felt a time when someone used their closeness to you to gain emotional energy from you? Yes, I'm sure you have. Now here's another question for you: have you ever used your closeness to someone to gain emotional energy from them? Oooh. Yes, most of us have to admit to that at some time or another as well, I guess.

Vampires and tidal waves

Vampires

The myth of vampires may not be so far from the truth. There are some people we meet in life who are so thirsty for energy that they will try to suck it right out of us, whether they mean to or not. Now I am not suggesting you hang garlic around your neck and carry a wooden stake in your hand, but it is useful to be aware of these kinds of exchanges. There are ways in which we can protect ourselves from being 'vampirised', but firstly we need to notice that it is happening – yes, it's our old friend 'awareness' again. Someone can only take energy from us if we allow them to. If we choose not to allow it, we can protect ourselves by imagining we are surrounded by a force-field like in Star Trek that they cannot penetrate. We could walk away from the situation, which is not such a bad choice; if there was a real live vampire in front of us – that is what most of us would do! Let's face it, we'd probably turn around and run like hell.

Tidal waves

Tidal waves are at the opposite end of the scale to energy-sucking vampires. These people have so much energy that they flood and engulf others with it. It is marvellous that someone feels they want to burst their energy out all over us, but it is often because they don't have any control over it and it is just chaotically gushing out all over everywhere. By sharing a load with us, they may find some relief, much as drug addicts often enjoy recreational drugs more if they have someone to share them with.

Being with a tidal wave can be inspiring and exciting, but coping with someone who has a huge excess of energy can use up a huge amount of our own energy and leave us as drained as having been too near to a vampire. Energy is not something that can be stored or destroyed, so if someone dumps more energy on us than we can comfortably handle, we're going to have to find something to do with it all. Being with someone who has far too much energy may be a bit like winning a million cans of beer: great in principle, but where are you going to put them all?

Allowing energy to flow

It is natural for energy to flow constantly: the more we allow energy to flow through ourselves and the people in our lives, the more potential for joy is created. Look at the ways in which energy moves around the planet. Nature stores energy in relatively small amounts, such as the fat in an animal's skin for hibernation or nuts for squirrels to munch on, yet even in the earth's core energy is always circulating and occasionally bursts out at the surface if it is bottled up for too long. This is the natural way to use energy – allowing it to flow through our lives, giving and receiving energy with other people, managing it in a balanced and sensible way so that it works for us and for the people in our lives.

Where we put our attention is where our energy will flow, so if we put our attention on difficulties in our relationships and our life, that's what the energy will fuel. However, if our attention is on loving and positive connections, that is what the energy will fuel. Make it your mission to use your energy to create the kinds of relationships and life you want. If you direct your energy in a very focused and clear way, you can use much, much less of it and still get the job done. Sometimes, using tiny amounts of focused energy can move mountains, whereas masses of unfocused energy would not have moved even a single stone.

Exchanging energy in balance

People whisperers only give as much energy as the person they are with can take and only receive the amount of energy that they in turn can handle healthily.

Be aware that some people will need you to tone down your energy levels for them to be comfortable or be able to cope with you, and others may need you to increase your energy levels for them to become engaged and involved in what you are doing.

Things to do:

1. Get into this 'energy thing!' It is so interesting. Start to develop an awareness of your own energy levels at various times and in various situations.
2. Develop an awareness of when people are attempting to draw energy off you or when they are engulfing you like a tidal wave with too much energy. Take steps to be responsible for your own energy levels, without being tossed around by others.
3. Remember that the Universe is full of energy, and that includes the air: if you need more energy, take a few moments to focus on your breathing and consciously breathe in some energy, allowing it to spread out through your body.
4. Avoid boosting your energy by simply borrowing it. Eating sugar and taking in caffeine are temporary ways to borrow energy. They give you a boost but you will have a lull again some time after, where you are in deficit.

As we have seen, energy, love and rapport are key ingredients for creating vibrant, fulfilling relationships in all aspects of life – work and play. But even as we use these ingredients to strengthen our bonds with others, it is important to recognise our differences, as we shall see in Secret Seven.

Secret Seven:

Get into Other People's Shoes

Every Person is Different

Every single person is different – that much is obvious. Yet, how often do we resist the fact that someone else thinks, behaves, talks or believes something differently to ourselves? We may think that we are always accepted exactly as we are, and that we readily accept differences in others, but if we look deeper, we soon realise that it is almost universal for people to have reservations, annoyances, doubts or judgements around others.

However, when we really and truly accept that others are different, the whole communication process becomes wide open, and once the process is wide open, anything is possible, because space has been created by removing those obstacles that formed resistance. Once there is no resistance, everything and anything is free to flow in and out of the interaction between ourselves and others; all things become possible. There really is great power in totally accepting someone for their own uniqueness.

Successful people whisperers recognise, accept and delight in the uniqueness of every single person on this planet, which means that they are attuned to everyone's individual characteristics and keep these in mind whenever they communicate.

In a loving relationship, totally accepting the other person means that infinite love, tenderness and intimacy can flow into our connection with them. In a work situation, total acceptance of someone enables all manner of business opportunities, possibilities and creativity to manifest themselves. Once a person has been accepted as they are, their attitude may soften.

Accepting Ourselves as Different

Accepting others as different begins with accepting that we ourselves are different. This can be a very challenging thing to do, because from birth onwards we are programmed to conform. From an early age we are made to feel uncomfortable in many situations for expressing our uniqueness. Particularly in situations such as those at school, we may try hard to fit in with the 'in-crowd' and to avoid being the one on the outside of the gang. When we conform to the gang we squash our individuality. We do this to ourselves and we attempt to do it to others too: at school, anyone standing out from the crowd is a prime target for harassment and bullying, because they are daring to express their 'difference'.

In adult life we may still come under pressure not to express our uniqueness. In the workplace we can become subject to the rigours of the company culture, to toe the line, not to make waves, not to be a maverick, not to rock the boat. Companies need rogue monkeys and original thinkers, but their presence is usually discouraged and, in some cases, feared. It is worth noting, however, that the great achievers in life are often those who do the things that others say are impossible, and in so doing they dare to express themselves, their uniqueness and difference.

Ask yourself:

◆ If you could express your uniqueness in any and every way you wanted, how would you be different to how you are now?
◆ What would you wear?
◆ What would you say to people?
◆ What would you do with your time?

Celebrating Uniqueness in Other People

When we accept someone as being different, we approach them with an openness that means we notice more about that person. As a result of perceiving more about someone we can begin to communicate with them in a way that works better for them and, as a result, better for us too.

Think about someone with whom you have an intimate relationship, or someone at work. Think about the ways in which they are different to you that you find challenging to accept. But if they didn't have those aspects to their character, surely they wouldn't be who they are today? The uniqueness of these people may be one of the reasons why we attract them into our lives. If there is something about them that is challenging for us to accept, perhaps we could appreciate that they have come into our lives with a gift for us: that gift may be the opportunity for us to expand and learn from them. Once we can fully accept someone we find challenging as simply being different to us in their ways, they will either miraculously change, quietly leave our lives or we may even become far more intimate and close to them.

Acceptance enhances communication

Once we accept that each person is different and unique, it follows that we would benefit from communicating with each person slightly differently. If we were to talk to everyone in the same way, we are apt to get punched, ostracised or leave others in a state of utter confusion. With some people it is very obvious that we need to take a different approach than the norm. The key here is being true to who we really are, allowing the other person to be who they really are, and speaking in a way that honours both of those realities. If we do this, we almost don't need to know the techniques and the details of 'how'.

Learning from variety

The uniqueness of everyone can be a vast source of helpful information, as it is sometimes easier to see how other people behave, think or do things in ways that make life difficult for them, than it is for us to see how our way of doing things is making life harder for ourselves. By watching the people in our lives doing, being, thinking and behaving in ways that are different to us, we can also see them do things in ways which work better than how we do them. And when we see people doing things that work well, we can experiment by emulating them to see if this behaviour will help us.

Things to do:

1. Celebrate your own individuality and celebrate other people's originality. Pay close attention to the ways in which at least three other people in your life are fascinating, amusing, impressive, sad, inspiring, unfathomable, unbelievable, incredible and lovable. Once you start looking, you will be amazed!
2. Think of a few ways in which you are totally unique and different from anyone else you know. If you can't think of anything, start exploring how you might be if you were free to be or do things exactly as you wanted. How would you be different from others if you allowed yourself to be?
3. Think of someone who does something that you find annoying or challenging. If you changed the way you viewed their behaviour, would you feel differently about them? For example, instead of finding their behaviour 'annoying', how would you feel if you simply relabelled it as 'expressing their uniqueness'?
4. Start looking at everyone you come into contact with and seeing how they express themselves by the clothes they choose to wear. Even when they dress to look similar to others there are still little badges of uniqueness, such as their jewellery, their hairstyle, shoes, or the way they present 'themselves' to the world.
5. Take a look at a housing estate of uniformly built houses. Notice how, despite every house being built the same, the inhabitants have displayed endless imagination in making their house represent something of their uniqueness and identity. This may be achieved through neglect, a mini-version of the maze at Hampton Court palace, an amusing array of gnomes or by adding stone cladding, grand entrance gates, or a portcullis and battlements!

Wearing Another Person's Shoes

To accept that everyone is different and unique is a useful aspect of people whispering, but to really take this approach further, we need to 'step into the other person's shoes'. Not literally, of course, but we can metaphorically step into someone else's shoes by seeing, feeling and experiencing what life is like from that person's perspective. The people whisperer is adept at seeing things from another's point of view and understands the value of taking on information from different angles; he or she walks in other people's shoes in many situations, increasing the ability to understand, empathise and create great rapport and closeness.

Have you ever wondered why someone does what they do, says what they say or believes what they believe? If you slip into their shoes you may begin to find out. Every one of us has had a unique set of experiences and we each have our own way of responding to all that happens to us. There are many examples of people who know someone really well and have been together in an intimate relationship for decades, and then suddenly their partner does something completely out of character and surprising. Wearing another person's shoes can be useful in so many situations – if we are in a dispute with someone, if we are making love with someone, if we want to motivate someone, if we wish to sell something, or to nurture and help someone to learn. Wearing another's shoes can give us insight, understanding, compassion, detachment, empathy and make us more loving.

Wearing someone else's shoes in a dispute

How many times have you found yourself digging into a position in an argument? The other person digs into their position too, and the stage is set for you both to expend (a polite way of saying 'waste') energy battling for your different opinions as though your lives depended on it. Well, don't worry – most of us do it.

What can change the whole dynamic of an argument, almost in an instant, is if we see things as the other person sees them; feel what it is like for them; hear what is being said through their ears; in short, wear their shoes for a moment. Suddenly the dispute will look different. The more we can ask someone to describe how it is for them so that we understand their view, the easier it will be to let go of the argument. This doesn't mean that we agree with them or have to change our opinion (though we may end up doing this). Simply, by looking at the issue from another angle, we will begin to disentangle things, much as, if we wanted to untie a knotted rope, we would turn the knot around to see where would be the best place to start loosening it.

Wearing someone else's shoes in a dispute, especially with a loved one, takes great courage and awareness. It is even more difficult if we feel that we are being criticised or attacked for something. But what sounds like personal criticism is often not that at all, and once we are in the other's shoes we can begin to take the defensive-aggressive 'you' out of the picture, as we realise the criticism is not personal.

Making love

Let's pick a nicer pair of shoes to slip into: how about making love? What is it like for the other person, the way we kiss them or the way we touch or stroke them? If we were them and feeling what they are feeling when we touch, kiss, stroke, tease or join together, what would it be like? How would we want it to be? What ways might make it more pleasurable or interesting for them? As your hand touches their body, imagine it is touching your body; as your mouth kisses their mouth, imagine what that feels like to the person you are with.

Swapping shoes to gain support or motivation

If we want to gain someone's support or motivate them to our cause, we can help ourselves greatly if we step into that person's shoes and see how they might be able to benefit from the situation. What would make them really want to walk the extra mile for us? How do they view us in this situation? Do they feel that we have their interests at heart? We can look for ways in which they might want to gain from the situation, which would also help us, so that we can combine their agenda with our own.

Making a sale

Similarly, were we wanting to sell something, it would help our sale along if we understood what made the potential buyer tick. By stepping into their shoes, we would have a clearer under-standing of what would make them think they needed our product, of how they were responding to our sales pitch and how we might pitch it differently to match what is happening internally for them. The more we can slip into another person's shoes and gain insight into how it is for that person, how the person thinks, feels, sees and hears, the more empathy and understanding we will have. Even slipping into an unpleasant, smelly pair of shoes (metaphorically speaking) can help us to understand why someone is acting in an unacceptable, hurtful, yobbish or antisocial way. That doesn't mean we condone their behaviour, but at least we will understand what is driving it.

Derek's Story

Derek enjoyed a high-level management position with an international bank. He was very successful in his work capacity and very effective at managing and leading the people in his team. But Derek was not so successful at relating to his teenage daughter and this was starting to make him feel uneasy even whilst he was at work, interfering with his concentration, eroding his self-confidence and making him feel edgy for much of his time in the office. In fact, the situation had become so bad that Derek and his daughter didn't communicate directly at all: their communications now all took place via his wife.

When Derek talked about the situation during a workshop with me, he was clearly upset, but more than that – the more he talked about it, the more I could see how much brooding anger he was harbouring. One of the issues that he talked about the most was the disgusting, messy state of his daughter's room, which really did seem to drive him mad. I asked Derek how he thought his daughter might feel about their relationship and how she might perceive him and the way he acted when she was around him.

He looked almost shocked by the question: he really hadn't thought how it might be for her or what she might think of the way he treated her. His response was something like, 'Well, maybe she feels unloved and unwanted by me and thinks I don't even like her. I guess she's withdrawing because she sees the way I am as being too bossy and angry with her all the time . . . blimey, that would explain a lot!'

I asked him what he might alter to help her feel different about him and his answer was very simple, 'Well, I could see things from her point of view and let her be how she wants to be. Maybe stop being "Mr Angry"', I suppose, and – if she wants to live in a room that's a tip – that's up to her, I don't have to live in it!'

I didn't even need to hear whether Derek's relationship with his daughter had improved after that session: there was such a profound change in his face, body language, energy and emotion in the instant when he put himself in her shoes that it was very moving for everyone present. There was no doubt that the father/ daughter relationship had changed from that moment on, before they were even together again in the same room.

A third position: wearing a 'fly on the wall's' shoes (don't say yuk!)
Normally we wear our own shoes. If we think about it, we can attempt to wear the other person's shoes, which is called 'second position'. The third position we can take up is that of an outside observer, like a fly on the wall. This gives us another angle to view things from and is the most objective position to be in. I am not suggesting you buzz around the light fitting and take an unhealthy interest in waste products left on the pavement: the fly on the wall is like an observer looking in, without taking any part in the proceedings, aside from watching them. This is a way to get to see what is happening between ourselves and other people, without taking either side.

Of course, it would be a miracle if we could look at things totally objectively, as everything we think, say and do is the product of years of conditioning. However, being willing to look at something from the outside will nevertheless afford us a fresh perspective – another angle from which to look at the same diamond, if you like. The advantage of taking up this third position is that it can loosen up our thinking and allow us to create new input or solutions, or even to let go of some of our unhelpful thoughts that might have been preventing a situation from progressing.

Positive Intentions

It may be hard to believe sometimes, but everything that anyone does is motivated in some way by a positive intention, from their point of view. However misguided their motivation for doing something may appear, somewhere deep in the recesses of their brain is a good reason for their doing what they are doing, even if that may not seem like a good reason to us at all. It is important to realise that, most of the time, people's positive intentions for what they do or say are unconscious: they are motivated by the intention but they aren't necessarily aware of it.

If we can wear another person's shoes and thereby discover that person's positive intention for their behaviour, we will have taken one huge leap of consciousness for humankind. Once we realise what is motivating someone to do something, and we appreciate that the person believes their actions to be positive in some way, the easier it is to deal with the situation. Certain behaviour can be easy to understand; for example, when a baby (or an adult!) yells and throws his or her toys out of the pram, the positive intention may be that the baby hopes to get more attention and love. Sometimes it may be slightly more difficult to discover the positive intention, for example when someone makes a cutting remark that makes us appear small, their positive intention may be to make themselves feel more important, significant and lovable in relation to ourselves. Other types of behaviour are especially difficult to understand in terms of their positive intention, for example, that of a sadistic tyrant who convinces the population to turn into genocidal maniacs against the people of their neighbouring countries. Nevertheless, those who have behaved in this way will have had a positive intention hidden in there somewhere, albeit something that is difficult to understand and hard to believe.

Things to do:

1. Practise wearing someone else's shoes in a situation such as a dispute, especially where you are really adamant about your view being right.
2. Look for the possible positive intention behind what people say or do.
3. Practise being a fly on the wall and looking in at yourself and someone else whilst you interact.
4. Put yourself in the other person's shoes when you want them to buy into an idea or commit to something. If you can find out what they want and combine it with what you want, you will be blessed with great success.

Stepping into other people's shoes will help us to see the world from their perspective, but it is equally important to respect the boundaries between us. At times it may seem that our differences are insurmountable or conflict inevitable. On these occasions people whisperers deploy the skills described in Secret Eight.

Secret Eight:

Create Healthy Boundaries

In order to build relationships based on mutual trust and respect, successful people whisperers understand the value and necessity of creating and keeping healthy boundaries. People whisperers also accept and abide by the boundaries that other people put in place. The boundaries themselves can be about all sorts of areas of life: they can be about behaviour; they can be about saying certain things; they can be about our sense of personal space; they can be about our finances or our use of time. They may be about how we express love and how much work or what type of work is acceptable to us. They may be specific, such as what time our teenage son has to be home at night and how loudly he can play his horrendous music, or whether our boss can ring us at home on a Sunday morning.

Think of a boundary as a permeable membrane (you remember biology lessons at school). Boundaries work by the process of 'osmosis' stopping certain unwanted things from passing through, whilst allowing acceptable behaviours and loving communication to pass through to us from others. Metaphorically speaking, boundaries are lines drawn around whatever we feel is acceptable to us, physically, mentally and emotionally. They are not barricades or walls, but represent a reasonable way of saying to others that 'This is what is acceptable to me' and 'That is not'. They can therefore be a very tricky area for people and may be disrespected in some parts of our lives. In intimate relationships, for example, where there is closeness and deep knowledge of the other person, it is very common for boundaries to be violated (although that sounds like a strong word).

Some people will test our boundaries quite determinedly. In these cases we have to hold fast, control our emotions and know where we have drawn the line on what is acceptable to us. Once the pressure is off, we can always review our boundaries and consider whether or not they are still appropriate or necessary. If we allow someone to destroy our boundaries, the resulting ill-feeling will not help the other person in the long run and certainly won't help us ... unless it teaches us to hold fast next time. People who refuse to accept our boundaries are saying something to us about how they don't respect us as individuals.

Meeting resistance to boundaries

When we establish boundaries it doesn't mean that we are not being loving; we can still be very loving, but we are also helping someone else to see what sort of behaviour would be OK with us and what would be going too far. Boundaries are a kind way of guiding someone to behave in a way that is acceptable when that person is around us. When we establish boundaries in an open and understandable way they will help others to know where they stand, after which, respect and closeness can follow.

With some people we may need to mark out our boundaries in a particularly clear, emphatic way. To do this without bringing negative emotions up from inside of us when we set or reaffirm our boundaries can be challenging and require adeptness and skill on our part. It is normal to set different boundaries with different people in our lives: if we had set the same boundaries with our work colleagues as we had with our loving partner, the workplace could soon become a very confused place!

Boundaries are our human right

Everyone sets boundaries at their own level: some people can tolerate more of their life being encroached upon by others or can put up with less decorous behaviour than other people can. People whose boundaries have been disrespected many times may react by erecting impenetrable boundaries for themselves, as a means of defence against future attack. These people can experience serious emotional and mental problems as a result of the lack of respect that has been shown to them and their boundaries.

Certain people in our lives, such as those who are dominant or vulnerable, or those with whom we are in close intimacy, can make it quite difficult for us to believe that we are allowed to set boundaries or to say 'no' to something. Peer pressure is a very common way for people to transgress our boundaries. Everyone will be familiar with jibes such as 'Go on, have another drink, you lightweight', or 'Everyone else will be going, you've got to come, what's wrong with you?' If someone is pushing against our boundaries, that person is confirming that we still need the boundaries in place. When we set new boundaries, people who are not accustomed to them may react in ways that can be challenging and uncomfortable for us. They may try to make us alter or erase our new boundaries using any approach they can, ranging from anger and intimidation to increased tenderness and softly-softly methods.

Being consistent

One of the keys to maintaining boundaries successfully is communicating them to other people in a way that they understand. It is no good setting boundaries, keeping them to ourselves and then slicing someone's head off when they overstep the mark – the poor now-headless person didn't know the boundary was there until it was too late. So we have to be consistent if our boundaries are to work. If we chop and change our boundaries with someone, that person will not know where they stand and become either very jittery or disrespectful around us.

Although we need to be consistent for our boundaries to work, that doesn't mean that they are written in stone and cannot be altered when our relationships or circumstances change. The thing about boundaries is that they need to be integrated into everyday life, and play a natural and healthy part in it, but not be over-focused upon or ignored . . . Balance is a key word with boundaries, and having boundaries can help to maintain balance in our lives. Boundaryless relationships are usually more dysfunctional than those in which both partners know where they stand, causing partners to be defensive or aggressive or both, in order to protect themselves from being 'abused'.

Remember that boundaries are not only about our direct interactions with other people: we have to set boundaries for ourselves too about things such as what is acceptable behaviour for us, how we manage our appetites for fun, food or sex, how much we work and how much money we are healthily able to spend.

David and Jan's Story

David and Jan were brother and sister. In many ways they had always been very close. Unfortunately, their closeness seemed to make David think he could say whatever he liked to Jan and that she would just take it, which she always had – for the first sixty-three years of their lives together anyway! Clearly David and Jan had no idea about the need for establishing respectful boundaries between them. They probably hadn't needed boundaries as small children growing up so closely together, but now as adults in their sixties, they were in danger of losing each other for good.

When Jan spoke to me, she was very upset about some very personal comments David had made to her about her husband and one of their daughters. Jan and her family had been invited to spend Christmas with David's family but because of what had been said, she did not want to go. Yet felt she couldn't say 'No' for fear of offending him or because he might 'lay into her' if she explained how she felt. Her only solution, as she saw it, was to duck out altogether and not get in touch with him at all, hoping the whole thing would blow over, somewhat like an ostrich burying its head in the sand.

I asked her to think about what she wanted to do about Christmas and what would be most comfortable for her. She said she didn't feel she wanted to visit David, so I suggested that she call him and decline the invitation, but also let David know that she was hurt by what he had said, in a totally calm and emotionally uninvolved way. To achieve this, I suggested she wait however long it took until her body felt still inside, and that while she made the phone call, she focused constantly on the inner stillness in her body. Since she was afraid that her brother would lay into her, I suggested that when she spoke to him she could calmly say what she wanted to say and then tell him that she did not feel that it was appropriate to discuss it any further with him at that time.

Jan took a few deep breaths and made the call in my presence. She was calm, focused, unemotional and clear; she laid out the facts and avoided apportioning blame: she was brilliant. Jan had set her first healthy boundary with her brother after sixty-three years of feeling like his much-loved punch-bag. What a relief! David's reaction was one of regret, surprise, apologies and a few tears: he had probably never realised how his unbridled comments had hurt the sister he loved so much. David went quiet for a couple of weeks after her call whilst he regained his equilibrium, but Jan held her nerve and finally they began communicating again, now with the respect and adult boundaries in place that Jan deserved.

Things to do:

1. Start thinking about what boundaries you already have in place with the people with whom you are close. Do those boundaries work, or do you need to change or reinforce them? Experiment with putting a couple more small boundaries in place about relatively minor things, such as who makes the coffee in the morning, etc.

2. Explore what boundaries you may need to set for yourself. Consider those areas in which you have the fewest boundaries and ask yourself what underlying needs are being met by your allowing those areas to run amok. For example, overeating may be a way of meeting the need to feel more loved. Indulging a rampant sexual appetite could be a way of meeting the need to feel more loved. Or, spending too much money visiting Dr High-Street for a spot of retail therapy could be a way of meeting the need to – you guessed it – feel more loved . . . Is there a pattern emerging here?!

3. Begin to put small boundaries in place if you need to. But be aware that if you are not used to setting boundaries, it may be challenging at first to do this without getting emotionally involved. For example, you may feel slightly aggressive or edgy about it.

CREATE HEALTHY BOUNDARIES

PERSONAL SPACE

Personal space is an interesting concept. Have you ever been on a crowded beach in summer looking for a patch of sand on which to set up 'camp?' Think about the way the people on the beach have spread themselves out and how they set up those temporary territorial areas. What makes you walk along the beach carrying your swag and rejecting certain spots? And then finally . . . what makes you pick a particular spot?

It is a similar phenomenon whenever we walk down a crowded shopping street. Isn't it amazing how rarely anyone bumps into anyone else? And when someone does bump into us and breaks that unwritten law of crowded shopping malls 'thou shalt not bump into anyone', we feel affronted and give them a grumpy look, or we apologise immediately, assuming we are the one who has broken the unwritten law and done the dirty on them.

People whisperers are aware of their own personal space and are equally aware of the personal space belonging to other people; they show respect by keeping an appropriate and comfortable distance for each situation and each individual.

Your personal space

What does your personal space mean to you? Perhaps it is a safety zone around you or an invisible skin. Clearly, society has a generally agreed rough guide to personal space, but within those guidelines, everyone has their own feelings about what their personal space constitutes. Depending on the kind of person we are with, our sense of the personal space we need changes. Through reading the signals given off by a stranger's body language and attitude, normally we will unconsciously know what distance needs to be kept between us. Unfortunately, some of the most uncomfortable train, plane and bus journeys can be the result of having to be nearer to a certain person's personal space than you feel is right!

My Story

I was unfortunate enough to have a driving instructor who liked to sit with his arms across the back of both seats and move his face in really close to me to talk while I drove. This was very uncomfortable, as it was high summer and the poor chap had rather noticeable B.O. and halitosis too . . . I learned to drive with my head out of the window, and it sure was an incentive to pass my driving test first time!

We can all tell intuitively what space we need. It can feel wonderful to allow some people close into our personal space and, if we both feel comfortable, this can be a subtle way of exchanging energy and love.

Using body space

We can use our awareness of body space and where we place our body in space, relative to other people, as a way of interacting with them. For example, standing well back from someone could be telling them that we want to keep our distance from them. On the other hand, some people will invade our personal space in order to appear intimidating or dominating, almost as though they are threatening to take up our space in the world. Yet, paradoxically, standing close into someone's body space can also be a way of sharing intimacy and warmth with someone: it all depends on how it is done and with whom!

The angle of the body also has an effect on what we convey to others. If we stand facing square on to someone, we are fully engaging with that person. This angle can also be used as a dominant position. If we stand with the body at a slight angle away from the person we are talking to, that person may feel more comfortable, but there is a danger that that person may feel that they do not have our full attention.

Things to do:

1. Become aware of what distances feel comfortable when you next talk to different people, and start to sense what the right distance

appears to be as far as the other person is concerned. Pick up the subliminal signals that tell you it is OK to be nearer to that person, or that you need to give them a little more space.

2. See how people position themselves in relation to you. For example, next time you stand in a queue, notice how you can feel the presence of the other people in it and whether it is uncomfortable when they stand too close to you.

3. Be aware of when someone, often a big person, uses up your body space to be dominant or intimidating. Once you realise they are doing this, it no longer has power over you; it may just make you chuckle!

WHO IS IN CONTROL HERE?

Healthy boundaries and a respect for personal space play valuable roles in our relationships, but as we have seen, boundaries and personal space are also areas in which some people may attempt to control and dominate us. In fact there are many areas of human interaction where control and dominance are unwelcome visitors. The people whisperer sees these patterns when they arise in people and does not engage in unnecessary control, dominance or subservience, choosing instead to maintain boundaries and simultaneously view every person as a valid, divine equal in their own right.

Although pecking orders exist within animal species everywhere and the human race is no exception, there are many areas of human interaction in which control and dominance are unwelcome visitors. People whisperers need to work around many different unhealthy forms of control and dominance in society.

Our fearful human ego often makes us want to control people and events in order to make our lives seem more safe and comfortable, and also in order to save ourselves from, largely imagined, pain or death. Although these driving factors of the ego are largely unconscious in our lives, they nevertheless influence our behaviour. Our fearful ego makes us believe that if only we can control events, and more particularly other people, we will be safe. But this is an illusion of *global* proportions.

Dominance and Insecurity

The most controlling and dominating people in the world are often the most insecure. If someone is attempting to control or dominate us, by seeing through their behaviour we can realise that they are probably being driven by fear and inadequacy. The controlling or dominating behaviour may be an attempt to make up for those aspects of their character in which they experience fear, lack or self-doubt.

Control and dominance at home

Practically all people play controlling, dominating, subservient or submissive games in some area of their lives, if not in most areas. In many intimate relationships when two people live closely together, it is 'normal' for control and dominance games to be played out. One partner may use their intimidating tone to get their own way; another may use the withdrawal of affection, intimacy or sex to gain their agenda; and yet another may play a weak, helpless victim role to gain control of their partner. Control can be a very slippery issue and in relationships it may be the person who *appears* to be outwardly submissive who is really the dominant partner, since that person may be using subtle means to manipulate their partner.

Control and dominance at work

Many kinds of dominance and control situations are found in the workplace. Our job position dictates to some degree our status in relation to the people 'above' and 'below' us. But if we want to enjoy authority, that does not mean that we need to control or dominate our team: it is possible to be a very successful leader without resorting to patterns of unhealthy control or domination. How to be a leader without waving the big stick of command and control is a hot topic in many of today's corporations, because it is quite a tricky skill to define,whereas waving a big stick is fairly easily done! One way to tell the difference between true leaders and bad leaders lies in the comments that they make. People find true leaders inspiring and motivating, encouraging them to do the best they can. On the other hand, bad leaders just don't generate the same enthusiasm. Which would you rather work for?

Handling power and authority

There are people who find it difficult to handle their authority over other people: this is a challenge of a different kind. To avoid jeopardising their relationships with their staff or their popularity, some people do not take up the leadership role that they are meant to play, choosing instead to be ineffective. Being ineffective is not the opposite of dominance and control, and being a leader or person in a position of authority does not necessarily mean that we are controlling or dominant. Do not shy away from using your authority as and when necessary for fear of being disliked, otherwise *you* are the one being controlled.

Things to do:

1. Are you a pack leader or a natural-born follower? Do you feel safe in the world at large? Explore areas of your relationships at home and at work in which you find yourself acting, or trying to act, in a dominant/controlling way. This might be through obvious domineering behaviour or sneaky, subtle behaviour. List the people whom you think you might be trying to dominate. Then ask yourself what you might be afraid of or insecure about that makes you act in this way towards these people.
2. For a brief period, try to let go of control of some area of your life in which you are normally quite controlling. (Of course it may be quite a challenge to admit to yourself that you are using controlling behaviour!) This could be at home, in the bedroom, at a club or society, or at work. See how it feels to let go of control; see where it takes you. Now practise extending the period of letting go of control.
3. Make a list of the people with whom you interact every day or every week at home and work. Ask yourself if you are allowing them to dominate or control you in any way, however subtle. For each person, list three simple steps you could take to help to redress the balance.
4. Practise becoming transparent in situations in which you are being dominated, rather than necessarily confronting the dominator.

Remember, someone can only really dominate you if you allow them to: even if they can *make* you do something, they cannot dominate your inner space if you don't give them permission.

5. If you are in a position of authority, experiment with the ways in which you could express your power positively. Remember that your inner state is what primarily affects other people: be sure not to load your authority with a negative emotional charge.

CONFLICT

For all that we may respect boundaries and explore issues of dominance and control, true people whisperers know that conflict is a natural part of life. People whisperers do not withdraw from unavoidable conflict, but do what they can to minimise the damage caused to themselves, to other people and to the Universe by this challenging aspect of life. It seems that conflict is a normal part of life. Even if you were an 'enlightened' being, you would be very rare indeed if you lived your whole life without experiencing some kind of conflict at some point.

What do We Mean by Conflict?

Conflict usually occurs when two opposing views are held, with both sides making a stand for what they feel is right. Conflict can be as much an internal experience as an external one; that is, we can be at loggerheads with ourselves over an issue as much as we can be in disagreement, big or small, with another person or people. It is often not the actual conflict that presents the problem, but how we handle it that matters. As we have seen, conflict is a natural part of life: birds do it, dogs do it, horses do it, people do it and even educated fleas do it! It is certainly true to say that it is natural for us to have different viewpoints and agendas to other people from time to time.

The benefits of conflict
Since conflict appears to be natural, we can deduct that it has some gift or value that comes as a result. Conflict that is healthily

expressed can clear the air, release tension and offer a way to move forwards; it can stretch us to find new resources and can be a place from which to build something stronger, including a stronger relationship. A tree that is battered by the wind will have stronger roots and branches as a result. (However, too much battering will stunt its growth and blow the fruit to the ground before it is ripe.)

Because conflict is usually uncomfortable, it can push us to learn and grow. Many of the most rapid and helpful discoveries and advances in science have occurred as a result of international conflict. Similarly, on a personal level, when we are stretched by conflict we may find extra resources, new strengths and skills within ourselves. Conflict in a relationship can likewise be a very positive sign: at least the other person feels comfortable, safe and empowered enough within the relationship with us to express themselves freely!

The downsides of conflict

Although it is possible to view conflict as serving some positive purposes, it can easily become destructive and unpleasant if it is not handled with care, respect and delicacy. Most people are very sensitive and easily hurt and, like a wounded animal, a hurt person is not always easy to reason with. Moreover, conflict uses valuable energy and may cause separation between people. It can be unloving and harmful, breeding distrust and hate, and causing lasting damage.

Since conflict is a part of life among people, we have various choices about how we deal with it. We can simply avoid it or withdraw from it. Unfortunately, avoiding or withdrawing from conflict can limit our progress through life and it usually has a way of catching up with us somewhere along the line. Alternatively, we can let it permanently affect us, which is not ideal! Or, finally, we can learn to handle conflict with skill as we would handle any potentially dangerous animal . . .'Yes: now that sounds interesting!'

Twenty-one ideas for Handling Conflict

1. State your point of view as clearly as possible, but keep your emotions out of it: don't be overtaken by anger, etc. Notice your emotions and be aware of them. Often, the wisest way to deal with conflict is to retain inner calm and strength, thereby affording you the best possible chance to resolve matters by meeting your opponent on middle ground.
2. Look for ways to go through the process and resolve it with the minimum damage caused, not only to yourself, but also to your opponents and to the environment.
3. Be aware of your strong attachment to needing to be right. It may be that there is no right or wrong in the situation; in fact, all sides may be in the right, depending on your viewpoint. Ask yourself: how can I be different in this situation that might help towards resolution?
4. Avoid dragging up the past. If you stick to dealing with the present both parties can move forwards.
5. Look for a way forwards, rather than going round in circles.
6. Remain as quiet and still inside and out as you can.
7. Practise stepping into the other person's shoes. See what it is that gives them the opinions, feelings or viewpoints they have. Step out of both your own and the other person's shoes and be an intelligent fly-on-the-wall: what is it like listening in from outside of the conflict?
8. Silently project a sense of unconditional love towards your 'opponent' through the cross-fire. Experience how this changes the dynamic, especially if there is a lot of hate and anger in the air.
9. Avoid making personal or insulting comments.
10. You may need to 'agree to disagree'. This is probably the most sensible solution in many of cases. The truth is, both sides will have a point of view that they believe in; otherwise they wouldn't be in conflict. Accept that you both see things differently and move on.
11. Avoid scoring points. Conflict is too costly to be a sport; it can cost more than money can buy.

12. See what happens if you simply say, 'Well, you may be right.' Now, that could be a very brave step!

13. Give them time to calm down in your company if possible. People who are difficult may need time to settle in, yet they often bring great rewards and gifts with them if you have the strength, love and patience to handle them.

14. Be sure that you understand exactly what your opponents mean and that they understand exactly what you mean. A great deal of conflict is unnecessarily caused by poor communication or lack of understanding of each other's message.

15. Know that however insane someone's standpoint appears, there is always a 'positive intention' behind every action or belief (as we saw in Secret Seven). Ask yourself if you really understand exactly what the other person's point of view is. What is the positive intention behind their taking this stand?

16. Remember that there is no shame in walking away from a conflict in which the opponent is superior to you and may therefore be able to inflict damage upon you.

17. There is no honour in fighting 'to the death' unnecessarily with someone over an issue. Be noble and find a solution that doesn't involve creating an outright victor; otherwise you may have created animosity that will return to haunt you one day.

18. See preserving the relationship and keeping goodwill with the other side as an important goal. If the outcome is one in which you have preserved or even strengthened the relationship, both sides are winners.

19. If you don't feel emotionally capable of dealing with something right away, be fair to the other person by giving them a commitment to talk again at a particular time on a certain day. Otherwise you are leaving them 'hanging'.

20. When you are speaking to someone to resolve conflict, speak from your heart: don't plan what you're going to say in your head too much, but allow the words you need to come 'through' you. Let yourself be guided and be in the flow.

21. Healing rifts between people is like healing a wound: it can take time and care, which means handling the wound with delicacy until it is stronger and avoiding stressing it with emotions such as impatience or anger.

Things to do:

1. Accept that conflict is a part of life. Do all that is possible to avert outright conflict, but be careful not to become a conflict avoider as this is not an honest way to have relationships (I know this, because I've done it!).
2. Look for the gift in any conflict and you will change the dynamic of the situation.
3. Watch how some people run their conflicts: become interested in people's 'conflict style' and then study your own conflict style. Ask yourself how could you alter the approach of your engagement in conflict so that it is less painful and bloody, and more productive, both for you and your opponents.
4. Let me wish you luck!

WHOSE 'STUFF' IS IT ANYWAY?

What often happens when two or more people come together is that the 'stuff' they each bring with them is brought to the surface. It may be that we can live reasonably well with our own baggage so long as no one else is involved, but when someone else turns up, and most especially in close personal relationships, our stuff surfaces and difficulties arise. What I mean by 'stuff' in this context is emotional baggage, junk that gets in the way, personal hang-ups and issues, patterns that cause difficulty, limiting beliefs etc. It is not necessarily easy for us to see what stuff we have, let alone to admit to ourselves that it is in there. And we may even complicate matters unconsciously by attempting to pin our stuff on the other person through all kinds of subtle means. The resulting entanglement can cause quite a lot of the confusion and upset, as we play out an unconscious game of denying or pretending that our stuff really belongs to someone, in the hope that we won't be found out and have to take responsibility for it!

People whisperers are aware of the need to recognise who is bringing 'baggage' into a conversation or relationship and are able to take responsibility for their own stuff, as well as recognising other people's baggage and not being burdened by it, choosing instead to handle such situations with sensitivity.

Emotional and Mental Toxins

Just as having a body full of toxins would inhibit our physical performance, so the build-up of emotional and mental 'stuff' inhibits our performance in and free-flowing experience of life. Sometimes we can be virtually crippled into inaction by the build-up of emotional and mental toxins formed since we were in the womb. Recognising that we suffer from emotional and mental toxins, and that they prevent us from realising our full potential, is the first step to becoming free of them. We may have carried some stuff in our system for so long that we cling to it and believe it is 'just how we are' or 'who we are', or an integral part of us and we think we would be nothing but an empty shell without it.

If we feel any emotions rise or feelings stir in our body, we know that we are bringing our own stuff to the situation in which we find ourselves. And once we know what stuff is ours, we can begin to see what stuff doesn't belong to us. If we feel 'wobbly' in a particular situation, we can ask ourselves whose stuff it is: ours or someone else's? The chances are it may be both! It is also worth recognising that if someone is being overly critical they are usually being motivated by their own stuff . . . Mind you, if we are bothered by their being critical, then that is *our stuff!* It can take a great deal of honesty and courage to admit that it is our stuff in the context of a relationship, as blaming another person often seems far easier!

What is 'running' you?
We think we are free men and women and live in a free society. But are we really free? Are we really freely choosing how we are and how we feel in every new moment, or are we bound by invisible chains that tie us to what we think we *should be* doing or attach us to our past? The truth is, unless we live totally in the present moment, with no thoughts of the past and no aspect of our character that is shaped by the past, we are indeed tied to it and therefore not entirely free. We all have patterns from the past: patterns of behaviour, ways of thinking and ideas and fears that

have been implanted in us, mostly by other people, who were also not free!

These unhelpful patterns are a major source of stuff. An example of a pattern might be that a dog bit us when we were two years old, so for the rest of our lives we are terrified of dogs. The examples are endless, and so is the amount of potential stuff we can collect over the years. As far as people whispering is concerned, the relevance of recognising our stuff is that it clears the way for us to communicate effectively and easily with other people, because then we are in a position to take responsibility for what we bring and consequently avoid cluttering our relationships.

By being aware of what triggers us to feel uncomfortable emotions or to feel physical unrest, we will shine a light on the sources of our discomfort. Once this light is present, we are free to step out of being run by the pattern because now we can see it. As we begin to identify limiting patterns in ourselves and to free ourselves from them, it will become easier to recognise the stuff that is not ours when we are with another person. This in turn means that we will not fall into the trap of taking on another person's stuff as our own, which will be a great help in making our communication clearer and more valid.

So Whose Stuff Is It, Then?

Let's say you are in a challenging situation and the other person just doesn't seem to be playing ball: they even think you are in the wrong! But you are sure that they are at fault and you may even start to become quite emotional (hurt, annoyed or whatever) about it. And so do they. So, whose stuff is it? Well, the way you are feeling about it is your stuff: the way they are feeling about it is their stuff. Nobody has the monopoly on the truth. Your truth is right – for you. Their truth is equally right – for them. How difficult that can be to accept, can't it?

Ask yourself:

◆ **Is it my stuff and I am trying to get them to take it on?** If you are feeling, saying or doing something, it is you feeling, saying or doing it, therefore it is your stuff!

◆ **Is it the other person's stuff and they're trying to get you to take it on?** If someone is feeling, saying or doing something, it is them feeling, saying or doing it, and therefore it is their stuff! They have choices – as you do.

◆ **Is someone trying to nail stuff on to you by saying 'You did this' or 'You did that' or 'It's your fault' or 'You made them feel like this or that?'** People will attempt to run all kinds of guilt patterns on you if they are unable to get you to take on their stuff. Watch out for someone trying to make you feel guilty for not taking on what is theirs.

If we realise that something is someone else's stuff, it may be best to say nothing about it to them. The most diplomatic way forwards is to recognise it but keep it to ourselves: we may be taking a risk by saying anything, as the other person may not respond too well to hearing us say, 'But, it's your stuff!' (Trust me; I've made that mistake myself!)

Things to do:

1. Start to notice when a comment or action by someone else has a negative emotional effect on you. Realise that it is your stuff that is making you feel that way: if none of your stuff resonated with what the other person said or did, it would pass through you unnoticed.
2. When you notice your stuff 'come up', acknowledge it inwardly and watch the feelings you have with interest. By doing this you will have altered the dynamic and the hold it has on you.
3. Be aware of when people try to make you responsible for how they feel. It can be quite challenging not to accept that responsibility, especially with someone you care about.
4. Avoid blaming, labelling or judging either yourself or anyone else for having stuff: anyone who has no stuff will probably be no less than a real live angel, and you don't see many of those hovering around these days!
5. Laugh at your stuff: next time you recognise a pattern coming up that you have seen in yourself before, have a chuckle to yourself at it.

6. Be compassionate, light and good-humoured towards someone you see being run by their stuff: it is a way of acknowledging that we are all in the same boat in some way or other.

DIFFICULT AND OBNOXIOUS BEHAVIOUR

Sometimes, we humans do challenging or mad things because of stress, inappropriate role models, issues of control over others or in order to hide our own fears. We may do crazy things in order to attract attention (when really we want more love) or from desperation, anger, frustration, lack of direction. We may need love and approval, be going through changes or, for no apparent reason whatsoever, we simply act out of character.

Difficult and obnoxious behaviour comes in all shapes and sizes, and can have a small irritating effect or be life-threatening. By difficult or obnoxious behaviour I mean anything from being grumpy or stubborn, through to being homicidal. I could go on and on listing ways in which humans have been found to be difficult and behave obnoxiously, as our species is so creative at this kind of thing, on an individual scale as well as globally. Personal relationships are a very fertile place, if not the most fertile of all, for this kind of behaviour. Whether we are in a state of conflict or not, expect the unexpected: even people we know well can be unpredictable sometimes! Therefore, people whisperers are adept at handling situations in which people display difficult behaviour and they know that *the person* is not *the behaviour*. People whisperers remain detached and love the person *behind* the behaviour, in the awareness that they may even be acting up because they feel safe and loved with us, and are therefore more able to express themselves!

◆ Are there any people in your life who indulge in difficult or obnoxious behaviour? Do you find yourself treading on egg-shells in what you say or do around them? What starts them off?
◆ How is it for you when they behave obnoxiously? Notice what happens inside you when someone close to you displays difficult behaviour.

- Would their behaviour seem obnoxious to someone in a different position to you? Would their behaviour seem obnoxious to them, from their point of view?
- Ask yourself: what are they trying to achieve or communicate through this challenging behaviour? It can be easier to understand someone's challenging behaviour if you see their reasons for acting in such a way.

Dealing with difficult or obnoxious behaviour in other people

It is worth realising that sometimes people may be completely unaware that they are being difficult or obnoxious. If we can make them aware of it in a way in which they can accept that their behaviour is affecting us, we may well find that they are surprised by the realisation. If possible, ask the person what it is really upsetting them, then hold the space and give them the chance to express their pain without judgement or reaction. Avoid 'rescuing' them or changing who you are in the hope that they stop doing whatever it is that they are doing (unless you do so temporarily until you are out of danger, and then leave them to it). If you alter your behaviour and they realise this, they have found a way to control you that they will almost certainly use again.

If it is an option, you could give them the space to be obnoxious on their own and, ideally, allow them to experience the consequences of their behaviour. Position yourself so that you don't have to experience the consequences of their behaviour. If you do need to be around, accept that you are choosing to live with their behaviour. Everyone has times of madness: keep things in perspective and decide how much madness is OK for you to live with.

Love the person behind the behaviour: the person, that is 'who they really are', is not the behaviour. As far as possible, stay centred and still: respond but don't react. Quietly send them love, despite the air being thick with 'challenge'. Say something to them such as 'When you do that I find it difficult to deal with', or 'When you are like this I feel hurt (afraid or whatever)'.

Dealing with your own difficult or obnoxious behaviour

Do you ever catch yourself indulging in obnoxious behaviour? Who or what is it that sets you off? At what point do you realise that the behaviour has overtaken you so that you are no longer in charge of yourself and a phantom has taken possession of you? Can you exorcise the phantom before it causes irreparable damage to your important relationships: that is, the relationships with yourself, your loved ones, other people and the Universe?

Remember that it is easier to avoid being overtaken by emotions when they are still quite small and quiet: once they grow to a size where they take you over, they are in the driving seat. Be aware of your emotions when they are still small; notice the tiny signals that your body, mind and feelings are sending to you.

Anger
Some people get angry very easily and frequently, in which case we may be better off leaving them to it. If we can remain 'transparent' in that we don't react to their outburst, often people's anger will go straight through us and carry on travelling, because it has nothing to hit up against.

If we ourselves are angry with someone and it is safe to do so, it may help the situation if we tell the person in a non-emotional way why we are angry. This will help them to understand where we are at and it also helps us to get stuff off our own chests. But we need to be sure to give the other party an opportunity to respond to us if necessary, without our descending upon them in retaliation.

We need to learn to manage our anger to have a ghost of a chance of forming harmonious partnerships with the kinds of creatures that are easily upset and hurt: such as human beings. In a sense, what right do we have to take our anger and frustration out on others, and what does it say about us as people if we do? If you start feeling angry, and can't let it go, leave whatever you're doing and give yourself some space.

Jealousy

Jealousy is almost as common as eating and breathing: at some point in life most people will experience jealousy of some sort. Jealousy is an emotion that can make us feel as though we are possessed: it is as if a demon had taken up residence in our body and mind. Feelings of jealousy need to be handled with delicacy, as these powerful emotions can lead to serious and harmful behaviour. If we feel jealous of someone else, it is up to us to explore and deal with those feelings ourselves; likewise, if someone else is jealous of us, it is for them to address their own feelings.

If we feel jealous, we can ask ourselves what underlying needs we have that are not being met, e.g. if we are jealous of a sibling who seems to receive more attention from our parents than we do, maybe we need to feel more loved or approved of. If we feel jealous that our neighbour appears to be much more comfortably off than we are, maybe it is the need to feel secure that is driving us.

Once we shed light on what is behind our jealousy, we have choices about how to feel. What we focus on expands, so if we focus on what someone else has and we don't, we will amplify that reality of 'they have' and 'I don't have'. The most powerful way to lay jealousy to rest is not only to accept that someone else has something we would like, such as love, money, attention or whatever, but actually to be pleased for them and rejoice in their good fortune.

Things to do:

1. Lay down on the imaginary psychiatrist's couch, and think about your childhood: what kinds of difficult or obnoxious behaviour were happening in your home when you were young? Explore this. It is your blueprint.
2. Pin-point some ways in which you behave that are difficult for yourself and for the people in your life (be honest, nobody is a saint . . . well, apart from saints). Think about what drives these behaviours in you: what is it you want that you are not getting?
3. Address your anger: let it out in a non-harmful way if you need to. Explore other ways to deal with anger, such as taking up meditation or yoga, which can dissolve a lot of negative energy.

Creating healthy boundaries and handling conflict creatively, by taking responsibility for our own part in it, are essential elements in communicating effectively. Fortunately, communication is about more than just fire-fighting and dealing with difficult emotions: it is also about creating balance for ourselves and others. People whispering offers many rewards, as we will see in Part III.

PART III

Reaping the Rewards of People Whispering

Secret Nine:

Balance Work, Life, Sex and Money

O ur natural state is to be 'in balance', where everything is effortless, where we feel centred and focused and everything we do falls into place with ease. But sadly it is actually quite rare for any of us to be in perfect balance, and there are so many ways to be out of balance in life. We are 'out of balance' when our emotions are shaky, when things do not stack up easily, when too much work has overburdened us, when life's difficulties are making us uncomfortable or when distractions make it hard to stay focused.

We may be knocked off balance by other people intentionally saying something to make us react, to control us, to get us to rescue them or to fulfil their own need for attention or love. Alternatively, we may be pushed off balance by other people without them meaning to do so, perhaps by them asking too much of us or by inadvertently saying something that has a detrimental effect on us.

And it is not only outside influences that can knock us off centre. We subject ourselves to strong desires and emotional ups and downs caused by guilt, fear, the arrival of bad news or frustration at reality not matching up to our expectations. We over-exert ourselves and push our bodies too hard.

Basically, our balance is upset when we 'overdo it' in any way, whether it is through our working, feeling, thinking or exercising too hard. We can also be knocked off balance by 'good' things in life, such as falling in love, coming into money or having a wild time. If we allow any of these influences to tip us too far, it can become quite difficult to right ourselves again, as the further we go off balance the harder it is to come back to being centred. The sooner we correct our auto-pilot back on to 'centre', the easier life can be lived.

It is not at all selfish of us to be concerned about maintaining our own life-balance. In fact, our efforts to stay in balance constitute a very generous act towards others, as when we are balanced we are able to give love and support to others more easily and with 'clearer' energy. The people whisperer is therefore aware of when life gets out of balance, and takes steps to re-centre.

BEING ADDICTED TO BEING OUT OF BALANCE

Bizarrely, it can be quite common for us to become addicted to being out of balance. Being out of balance gives us something to obsess about and use to create our own drama. It gives us something to talk about with others and is a way to attract the attention and support of people close to us. If we notice ourselves doing this, *great*, we've noticed: we can then make a conscious choice about whether to find a balanced position and take responsibility for our own needs.

It may sometimes be the case that we recognise when another person close to us is habitually out of balance and this seems to be benefiting them, but pointing it out to them may not help. What we can do is be loving and empathic, but without buying into their drama by giving it energy or attention, which may be unhealthy. Avoid helping them to carry their 'baggage'.

Realigning Your Balance

Living life skilfully is about making an almost constant string of minor (and sometimes major) corrections that bring us back into balance. This is how we unconsciously steer a car down a straight stretch of road: by tiny readjustments of the wheel. As a learner driver we may leave it too late and then have to make big conscious corrections, but as experienced and attentive drivers, we keep a better line and make constant small corrections unconsciously. The list below highlights some of the areas in which we may become out of balance, and suggests ways in which we can realign ourselves.

Emotions: Take notice when your emotions rise up. If you are aware of what is happening inside you, there will be less chance of your emotions being able to take you over. Stay with this and keep watching them: this will help you to stay more in balance.

Thoughts: Be aware of when your attention goes or you start thinking compulsively about something and your mind can't/won't/doesn't know how to stop thinking and let go of it. Again, by noticing what is going on in your mind, you will retain independence and balance.

Body talk: Listen to your body: if it is tired, let it rest. If it is hungry or thirsty, give it food or drink. If it reacts badly to something (like too much alcohol, chocolate, coffee, exercise, fresh air, exhaust fumes, work etc.), avoid exposing it to what it cannot handle. If it has excess energy to express, let it out! Run, play and dance: turn your energy loose (ideally in a way that is fun but also socially acceptable!). Illness is often a result of your body shouting at you to get it back in balance; it has probably been whispering the same message to you for a while, but it wasn't being heard.

Only bite off what you can chew: Sometimes life throws us into something that is difficult to handle and our balance goes right out of the window. But there are times when we unnecessarily enter more difficult situations or relationships with people than we can really handle and still remain balanced. Therefore, wherever possible, only bite off what you can chew.

Steps to Re-balancing

1. Once you have noticed you need to re-balance yourself, keep your awareness on what is happening in your mind, emotions and body.

2. If possible, go somewhere quiet or be on your own. Let your body be really still and quiet: this is a great way to begin the balancing process. Let your body lead the way to stillness and allow your emotions and mind to follow your body's example.
3. It may help to take a break or put some space between you and whatever is challenging your balance.
4. There is no point *trying* to force yourself back into balance. Being in balance is your natural state. Go into being quiet, watch your breath, give yourself space and wait. Gradually allow your natural balance to return.

Fun, Fun, Fun

Like balance, fun is a natural experience for us in life, but one that we sometimes lose sight of. Fun is itself an excellent tool for re-balancing ourselves, helping us to release the build-up of 'heavy energy' in us caused by meeting the demands of our modern adult lifestyles. Having fun is a great way to access the playful inner child, which we all carry within us somewhere. Recognising our inner child and letting it out to play helps to put things into perspective in our lives. Fun and play are clearly natural states and are something that animals do even as adults, especially mammals. Watch dogs, cats, horses or even cattle: assuming they have their basic needs met, they all have fun and play-times scheduled into their timetable of bio-rhythms.

Sharing fun with others is a fabulous way of creating or deepening bonds. Laughing together and reaching the lighter parts of life with someone is very healing and is a great way to lower barriers between people. Everyone has their own ideas about what is fun: what is yours? Everyone has ways to release their energy in different ways: be honest about what works for you.

When it comes to having fun, we may be afraid of what others might think. And as well as worrying about the opinions of other people, our own judgements may stop us from pursuing what might be regarded as a frivolous or childish activity. Notice if you are not having fun in a way you would like because of what others (or yourself) might think: go ahead, do it and be empowered by not giving a damn if you look a fool or not! Too much fun? You could say that it's impossible to have too much fun – and in many ways that is a great attitude to have in life. But if our need for fun becomes an addiction, like anything else, it may become a source of loss of balance in life.

Things to do:

1. Notice the next time you have one of those (probably) rare moments when you experience a sense of being totally in balance. Explore it, cherish it, indulge in it, be with it and let yourself become deeply familiar with it, so that through such familiarity, you will be more able to recreate it at other times.
2. Create a list of five people or situations that can knock you out of balance easily. Use this awareness to help you to feel prepared and centred if you are ever in that company or situation again.
3. Set aside regular times to re-balance yourself by having a break, resting and having fun. This could be for five minutes a day, one day a week, one week a year – whatever it takes for you.
4. Within the next six months, go ahead and do one fun thing you've never done and wished you had.

Sex

One of the most natural and effective ways to release energy, re-balance, connect with another person and have fun all at the same time is through sex. Sex is potentially one of the deepest and most wonderful ways for people to communicate and exchange energies. Unlike most other species, humans have been given the gift of sex not only to procreate, but also to enjoy as a means of connecting with one another.

Sex is an emotive subject, not least because it is such a powerful force within us. Since it is such a powerful force, many religions and societies have felt the need to control sex and give it a certain taboo. Unfortunately, this kind of cultural control of what is an instinctive and natural way to connect with each other has brought much fear, guilt and discomfort with it. Despite that, it remains as popular as ever (funny that!) and continues to bring much-needed intimacy into people's lives. Sex can be reduced to a functional, physical activity, but at its best, it can be one of the most rewarding ways to communicate with another person. There is little disagreement that sex within the context of a loving, intimate relationship is more deeply fulfilling than just plain sex.

The people whisperer appreciates that sex is a divine gift and a way of exchanging energies in the physical realm at a potentially deep level and is aware of what a powerful motivating force sex represents to people.

Depending on your beliefs and attitudes around the subject, sex can be many things:

Sex can be awesome	Sex can be wild
Sex can be gentle	Sex can be lonely
Sex can be a relief	Sex can be moving
Sex can be playful	Sex can be painful
Sex can be uplifting	Sex can be passionate
Sex can be loving	Sex can be boring
Sex can be beautiful	Sex can be exciting
Sex can make you feel open	Sex can make you feel closed
Sex can make you feel vulnerable	Sex can be disturbing
Sex can be selfish	Sex can be funny

Let's talk about sex
Because sex can be a taboo, embarrassing or uncomfortable subject to discuss, we don't always talk about our needs in a direct and understandable way. As a result of this, we can continue to feel disappointed with our sex lives. It may take courage to speak up and ask your partner to turn you on by wearing a fluffy pink tutu, yelling like Tarzan and swinging from the door handle before kissing your fingertips and saying 'I am yours', but hey, if that's what you need to get you going, you had better ask for it, because no one is going to be able to do that much guesswork for you!

Getting started on talking about a subject such as sex is often the hardest part. Once you and your partner know that it is safe and OK to communicate openly about the subject, you will be able to move forward together to new heights of experience. Talk in a way that frames things in the positive: that means saying things like 'This really turns me on' or 'That feels good to me'. Avoid criticism of your partner or they may close down very quickly. Remember that sex is a sensitive area for most people, so they can feel very vulnerable to negative feedback or criticism.

Ask yourself about sex:

◆ What signals do you give out about yourself sexually through your body language, the way you are and the things you say? How do you think other people read the signals that you give out?

◆ What expectations do you have around sex? Are these expectations realistic?

◆ Does sex cause you discomfort because of the fear of losing control of yourself or your feelings? Is that because the sensations of sex are overwhelming and that means someone else may take control of you?

◆ If you are in a relationship, what are you communicating to yourself or to your partner that may not be helping your sex life together? What could you communicate to yourself or your partner that might be more helpful?

Guiding your lover

It is most effective to teach your partner what you want from them by communicating through positive responses. Whenever they do something you like, phrases such as 'Mmm, that's good' or 'I love it when you do that' will guide them and help to create the kind of experiences you want to have. The most direct way of giving positive feedback is to respond in the moment. For example, if your lover's hand is somewhere you like, an approving sound from you will teach them they are on the right track. Similarly, if they go to somewhere not quite right, you don't need to say 'no' – just be quiet. This is a very clear way of teaching someone what works and what doesn't for you, and subsequently for them too. Most people want to please; they just need some help and encouragement in figuring out how. Of course some people are more receptive and quicker learners than others, so don't get impatient if your guiding or training doesn't get immediate results. If the way you are communicating isn't working, look for different ways to put across the same idea.

Making love with your whole self

What we are talking about here is communicating sexually with another person, but going beyond the body. It doesn't take much to have sex with just your essential physical parts, but then it doesn't give you much back either. Engaging the whole of yourself – body, mind and soul or real self – when making love with your partner will help both of you to reach greater heights of connection and intimacy.

To engage the whole of your body, focus on the different sensations in different parts of your body: sense what you feel in your legs, feet, head, chest or hands simultaneously during love-making. Let your awareness take you deeper into the experiences that your body is leading you through. To physically engage the whole of your partner, touch not only their body, but particularly their head, face and hair. People live mostly in their heads and feel that that is where 'they' are, so connecting with their head can help them feel that you are paying attention to them 'personally'. To completely connect with someone's whole body, try touching your lover's feet during lovemaking. This may make them feel as if their body is being totally embraced by you, literally from head to toe (not forgetting the interesting bits in the middle of course). To connect with your lover on a deeper level, you could look into their eyes during lovemaking. Remember that the eyes are the windows of the soul and this can intensify the sense of together-ness you both experience.

Be as present as possible with your partner: that means being aware of everything that is happening in you, between you and around you. It means dropping thoughts about whether to have chicken or beef for dinner, where to go on holiday or what to tell the neighbours in order to explain away all your squeals. It also means dropping fantasies about being with someone else or somewhere else. When you drop all the mental interference and are totally there in the moment, you open up the possibility of a far richer level of communicating experience for both yourself and your partner, since when you are fully present, they will sense it and be able to join you.

Things to do:

1. Ask yourself honest questions about what sex means to you and where those meanings come from.
2. Bite the bullet and start to find ways to have honest, open conversations about sex. Ask for what you want in ways that make it easy for your lover to want to respond.
3. Start training your partner using positive guidance: think of it as a long-term project. On the one hand you focus on how their training is coming along; on the other hand, you focus on your skills as a trainer and communicator.
4. Become sensitive to timing and moods: work *with* the nature of sexuality, instead of ignoring it.
5. Enjoy yourself! Explore sex as a means of experiencing a variety of deep physical, mental, spiritual and fun connections with another human.

Money

Along with sex, money is an area of our lives that can have a big influence on our state of balance. Money could be the subject of a whole book in itself (and probably is), but what we are specifically looking at here is money as a form of exchange and communication between people. Money is an amazing and often contentious concept that is all about people: without people, money would simply not exist. Money represents an agreement between people, a way of exchanging energy at a pre-agreed rate. Money is not really about paper, copper or gold; it represents our efforts and is a way of swapping one person's efforts for those of another person.

Money is a means for the Universe and other people to provide for us, so that we can live our lives without having to do everything for ourselves. In the West, we no longer have to grow all our own food, build our own houses, or provide for all of our other needs entirely by ourselves. The wonderful medium of money enables people to support each other so that they are free to pursue more focused and expressive lives, knowing that their particular contribution to society means they do not have to take care of all of their basics first-hand. Money may not be the answer to life's problems, but I have heard it said that money is a great lubricator in life! The people whisperer therefore understands and enjoys the mechanism of money as a means for people to exchange their energies, allowing it to flow freely and trusting the Universe to provide.

Some views about money
Money is seen:

◆ to cause trouble between people, but it is not the money that is causing the trouble, it is the people
◆ to be the answer to our problems, but the problems exist in our minds, because we perceive a gap between how we want things to be and how they actually are in reality
◆ to make us comfortable; there is no doubt that money can buy us a more comfortable hospital bed, but it won't necessarily make the pain in our body hurt any less
◆ to buy us a good life, but it cannot mend a broken heart, bring back a loved one or create inner fulfilment
◆ to afford us freedom, freedom from having to work, freedom to travel and to do the things we want to do; but true freedom is a state of mind and that comes for free anyway
◆ to bring us security, but it cannot save us from being a danger to ourselves. Besides, security is something of an illusion: we could have all the money in the world and yet our private jet could 'plop' into the ocean, never to be seen again!

Allowing money to balance and flow
So if money represents an exchange of energy and effort between people, what does it mean if money is not flowing easily into our

lives (or into our pockets, more handily)? Could it be that we are withholding our energy from someone, or is someone withholding their energy from us? If money is energy and we have lots of it, saving it up in a fearful way could be said to stop its flow, and energy that is not flowing is not serving or creating anything.

Doing something just for the fun of it and not for payment is not necessarily likely to bring us money: it becomes a hobby, not a paid job. In order to receive money for doing something we love, we have to let other people, or the Universe, know that we are happy to be paid for our services. We also need to be very clear with ourselves that our work has value and we deserve to be paid for it. If we do what we are passionate about and allow things to flow, money will usually follow. An ideal situation might combine doing what we want to do for money with meeting a need that people have. If they don't yet realise their need, perhaps we can somehow reveal it to them.

Money as a positive exchange

Do you appreciate the money you have coming in? If you do, more will probably follow. Since money is a way for people to exchange their energies, appreciating the money that we have is similar to expressing our appreciation of another person's efforts on our behalf, which will make them want to do more for us. If every time we do a job our primary motivation is our love of the job, we will do the job to a higher standard and people will notice this; then more people will want to hire us and money will flow to us. When money is handed over from one person to another it can be a loving exchange or a negative exchange: choose to make it the former.

Ask yourself:

◆ Which do you notice more – the people who have more money than you or the people who have less? How does this affect your take on life?
◆ Do you enjoy exchanging money with people as a way of saying 'thanks' for them giving you their energy or helping you? Do you allow money to flow freely in your life?
◆ What do you really need other than food, shelter and basic medical care? Can you think of all the rest as a fantastic bonus?

Enjoy money as much as possible, but remember to keep it in perspective and take a balanced approach to it. However much we have or don't have, it is all temporary and we can't take it with us when we die.

Adam and Nicky's Story

Adam and Nicky were a successful professional couple in their late twenties. They both earned good money, worked hard, played hard, owned their own home, and were very happy together and very much in love. Then, after about two years of living together and enjoying their life together to the full, the company Adam worked for was hit by the dotcom crash and he was made redundant from his job. As he was a high flyer he had no trouble finding new employment. In fact, he found a placement that was actually going to further his career more than his previous post could have done.

The only down side of Adam's new job was that it was more than two hundred miles away from where they lived, and Nicky's job in publishing was tied to their original location. Aside from which, they both loved where they lived and didn't have any desire to move. So Adam commuted to work during the week and came back home at weekends.

This arrangement worked OK for the first year or so, but as time went on Nicky began to feel the strain of snatching a few hours of intimacy at the weekends. And even those few hours at weekends were not giving them any real quality time together. Adam would arrive home very late on Friday evenings and was then tired out all day Saturday. Because he used to drive off again on Sunday evening to get ready for work on Monday morning, he would spend the whole of Sunday feeling tense and unable to relax, in anticipation of going again. Nicky explained to me in one of our coaching sessions how she felt more and more unloved and isolated in her relationship. After two years of this arrangement, her need for more intimacy led to her becoming interested in another man, and wondering whether to leave Adam in order to begin a new relationship with the other man.

Nicky and Adam had allowed work and money to push them apart. They had lost the balance in their lives and forgotten how important their relationship was and how much fun they had together. I asked Nicky if she had communicated how she felt to Adam in a way that he understood and she replied that she didn't think he realised what was going on – so probably not. I suggested she talk to Adam by speaking his language, using words and phrases that he would understand, and that she also hold the space and give him time to say how it was for him, without fear of a reaction.

They did talk about their situation and, as a result, when Nicky heard Adam's point of view, she realised just how inflexible she had been in sticking with her job when Adam had been forced to move on. As a result of this, she spoke to her employers who agreed to her working on a freelance basis from home, which meant that she would earn less money but have more free time. It also meant that they would be able to move their home to where Adam's work was based, thereby regaining the balance in their life and relationship at long last.

Things to do:

1. Start to enjoy money without becoming emotionally needy, knocked off balance or overly attached to it (no one said all the suggestions in this book were going to be easy!). Experiment with letting money flow in your life. This means being aware of how you allow it in and out of your life and the emotions you attach to those comings and goings.
2. Look at people who are successful or simply comfortable with money. Study how the ways in which they think, act and feel make money work for them.
3. Take a look at other areas of your life, such as relationships, in which you might be wasting energy, blocking energy, investing or expending it in non-worthwhile ways or allowing it to be drained from you. Does each area of your life give you a reasonable return for the investment of energy that you put in?

Work

One of the areas of life that is closely related to money and frequently knocks us off balance is that of work. 'Work' is a major four-letter word and one that takes up a huge amount of time in our lives. Our beliefs about work are highly significant in determining the quality of the lives that we enjoy, or don't enjoy. Work can be one of the most fulfilling and motivating aspects of our lives or it can be one of the most difficult and tedious areas. But if we weren't meant to work, there would be piles of food left out for us every morning by the food fairies, homes would build themselves, and all our other needs and wants would be met just by asking . . . (actually, that doesn't sound too bad!).

Work is an interesting animal and represents one of the major areas in which people whisperers can practise their art and thrive as a result of skilful communication. Work is almost entirely about other people, involving either talking to customers or dealing with managers, fellow staff or 'bosses'. Therefore, much of our experience and success at work is about our interaction with others.

Ask yourself:

◆ How do you see your work? Do you work for money or for the love of what you do? Would you dare to think you could work for the latter?
◆ How do you view other people in work? Have you ever made assumptions about people because of the work they do?
◆ If work brings meaning to our days, what meaning do you allow your work to bring to your days?
◆ Do you see the work you do as bringing value to the people who are at the receiving end of your products or services, e.g. the people who drink your beer, whose savings are increased by your company or who enjoy your plastic ducks at bath time?

Work can play a large part in expressing who we are, which is why successful people whisperers seek to work in fulfilling ways that bring a valuable contribution and make a difference to others, as well as to themselves.

Taking your 'whole self' to work

There may be aspects of ourselves – our personalities, thoughts and feelings – that we don't take to work. However, if we are not true to ourselves at work, we may also be holding ourselves back from realising our true potential. Take a moment to think about how you are in the workplace. Are there are any aspects of yourself that you don't take to work with you? Now think about how you are in your social circle or with loved ones . . . How do you differ and in which situation are you happiest? What would happen if you fully engaged with what you do at work? What if you were at your most brilliant, joyful, committed and friendly when you were at work? Do you realise that in all of these different situations, the common factor is 'you'?

We may find it hard to believe, but ultimately we all have choices about the work we do and we alone are responsible for how we feel when we do it. We really are free to bring all of our selves to our work: that means all of our attention, energy, focus, imagination and people skills. If we were to bring our 'whole selves' to our work, most of us would feel happier and freer, whatever workplace culture we were to find ourselves in.

Workplace Culture

Wherever we work, there will be some kind of culture, approach, atmosphere and attitude that goes with the territory. It is very easy to think that the culture is 'the company' and is therefore out of our hands. In truth, the culture is whatever the people within the company agree to buy into – and that includes *you*. In fact, we could go so far as to say that 'the company' only exists as an agreement between all the people who work there at any one time. A company is a group of companions; in a commercial context they are agreeing to produce certain goods or supply certain services together. The 'culture' and the 'company' are not separate from us: we are a part of them and we continue to keep them alive (or not!). Bearing this in mind, how do you view your own ability to change things at work? Do you realise that you really matter, you *do* count and your contribution *is* necessary? Why else would you be paid to do what you do?

Relationships in the workplace

Our success at work depends to a huge degree on the connections we form there with others. As we spend a large part of life at work, it has to be beneficial for all concerned if we get along well together and enjoy healthy exchanges of energy. To that end, the secrets of the people whisperer outlined in this book can be used to nurture relationships in the workplace.

Since no one is an island, remember that if we change our way of thinking, behaving or being, our environment and the people around us are also changed, even if those changes are simply in the way we perceive them; regardless of their rank, that means it is possible to influence people in the workplace upwards and sideways as well as downwards: in reality, everyone makes a difference.

Influence is something that spreads out in all directions, so don't doubt it goes upwards too! And if we ever find ourselves in a limiting situation where superiors don't allow us to expand, we can be confident that another, more suitable situation will manifest soon for us.

Things to do:

1. Imagine that you are an old man or woman, sitting in your favourite chair. Think about what you might like to have achieved if you looked back over your life: what contribution you would like to have made, how much fun you would you have had doing it and what kind of relationships would you need around you to bring it about.
2. Ask yourself what work you would do if you could really choose anything: dare to think it . . . and dare to ask what you might do to allow it to happen.
3. Look at some of the work-related relationships you have. Begin to make a difference for the better to one of those work relationships today, perhaps by a small gesture of kindness or appreciation.
4. Look at how much balance you have between your work and the rest of your life. How much time and energy is left over after work has taken what it needs?

By achieving balance in our own lives we create a firm foundation upon which to build balanced relationships with other people – which can lead to beneficial outcomes for all concerned, as we will discover in Secret Ten.

Secret Ten

Share the Path to Success

CREATING WIN-WINS

The people whisperer realises the benefits and value of ensuring that all parties gain from any given situation, and to that end always aims to arrive at win-win solutions. In a win-win, everyone walks away a winner, happy and satisfied; all concerned feel that they have benefited in a way that works for them. This is in contrast to more usual outcomes in which one person wins and the other loses, and consequently feels dissatisfied or denied something.

Since we humans can be very competitive creatures, we tend to lose sight of the potential cost of winning over someone and more often than not we forget the value of creating win-win situations. Win-wins promote growth, opportunities and positive energy.

Win-wins are a way to create allies: People with whom we create win-wins are more likely to stand by us in the future, because they know they can work with us and that we are the kinds of people who will consider their needs and their points of view, as well as our own.

Win-wins create positive energy: There is far more possibility of a feel-good factor when people create a win-win.

Win-wins create the possibility of new levels of relationship: By creating a win-win, we form a bond of mutual respect with the other party.

Win-wins feel good: Win-win solutions can create a sense of shared satisfaction, as they make both parties feel that they are cared for and important.

Win-wins bring the possibility of new creativity and opportunities: Because win-wins are about building bridges and new or renewed relationships, there is always the chance of taking these relationships into new areas. Once we have found common ground with someone, there are always other things we can create together.

Win-wins send the right kind of boomerang words and actions out into the Universe: Since win-wins are a positive and loving way to communicate with people, they send out loving and positive energy, which will return to us sooner or later. Every time we create a win-win with someone, that person takes the positive energy of that outcome with them and forwards our cause out in the world as a result.

How to Create Win-Wins

1. Set it up to be easy: the fewer obstacles you put in the way of finding a smooth flow that both parties can share, the better.

2. Let go of grim determination, anger, frustration or any other negative emotion and the need to be right at all costs. This is easy to say and not so easy to do, especially when you feel strongly about the matter in hand or you start digging into your position and don't want to budge.

3. Put yourself in the other person's shoes. See what they need to gain from the solution. See why it may be difficult to reach for them, and see where you can afford to be more flexible if they need more room in which to manoeuvre, especially if they have boxed themselves into a corner.

4. Ask the other person, your inner self or the Universe what the options are, or what else could help to make everyone a winner. Think of at least three options, even if only one seems viable.

5. Use your imagination in order to allow solutions to evolve for the benefit of all concerned. Our minds are pretty well limited to familiar patterns of thought. Allow your mind to be quiet and give your imagination room to do what it is good at: being imaginative!

6. Let go of any specific expectations you have about the outcome: there may be a number of ways in which you could gain what you need. By letting go of what the outcome *should* be, you widen the gap of possibilities. Remember that, whatever happens, none of this will matter to you in a hundred years' time, so why not let go of some of it now?

7. See if by giving the other person what they want you can get what you want too. It may not work that way, but sometimes, by giving, we can prompt the other person to give too.

8. In a difficult situation, ask the other party, 'How can *we* resolve it?' (rather than *you* or *me*).

Things to do:

1. Simple: look for opportunities to create win-wins! That way you can't lose!

2. Open yourself to the other possibilities of the situation instead of digging into your own position. Be aware of when you think you are creating a win-win, but you are actually creating a win-lose – in which you are the loser! This isn't being kind or charitable on your part, it is being a mug.

3. Stand back from the situation: if you look at any relationship problem from a different angle, or put a bit of distance between yourself and it, it will look different and certainly will feel different.

4. Imagine a life in which all of your close companions are winners, winning in win-wins . . . In what ways would your life differ from the way it is now? What would it take to make that imagined life a reality?

5. Most Importantly: be a gracious and good loser. That way you can't lose. We can't win them all, in the way we might like, but we can be gracious in defeat and we can find other benefits from not winning.

AMBITION AND DRIVE

Creating any kind of win, whether it be for ourselves, on behalf of another person or for all parties concerned requires that energy is channelled into the situation and two of the most effective ways to do that are through ambition and drive. People whisperers know the value of using healthy ambition and drive as tools to further people's journey through life and they therefore enjoy encouraging the flow of energy created as a result.

Ambition and drive contribute to the greatness of humankind

It is because of our natural bent for furthering ourselves that we humans have come so far in advancing ourselves, our society and our way of life. It is humankind's habitual ambition that brings forth the motivation to create, invent, explore, discover and learn: ambitious people have always been at the frontline of moving us forwards to new areas of our potential, both individually and collectively. When ambition is healthy it is a great motivator and encourages a flow of resources and energy through us that is highly constructive: ambition could be described as the desire to fulfil our greatest potential in life, whatever that may be. Whoever we are, and at whatever stage we are at in our lives, there will always be new ways for us to create, invent, explore, discover and learn.

Ambition is a greatly admired quality, especially in Western society. We tend to be very enthusiastic and supportive of people who 'go for it' and make things happen in their lives. Ambitious people who have risen up from humble beginnings are particularly held in high esteem. The idea of the self-made man or woman, or the person who dragged themselves up from the backstreets to go on to greatness, is something we hold up as an ideal. This is fine if we are ambitious too, but if we lack drive and ambition, or don't know yet where our real purpose in life lies, it can be very disheartening. As society seems to revere ambition, if we are not ambitious it can be easy to feel that there is something wrong with us.

However, there is simply not scope for everyone in society to be one hundred per cent ambitious one hundred per cent of the time: if we were all to pursue the same level of success – to get to the same hilltop or the same treasure – society would be out of balance and in conflict with itself. Moreover, the pressure to achieve can create personal tension, too, so if we have someone in our lives who does not appear to be ambitious, it may simply be that they need the space in which to find out where to direct their energies. This is also normal, so if you yourself have yet to find your driving ambition in life, let yourself off the hook!

Even if everyone eventually achieved their full potential through following their ambition, they would all end up in different places, at different levels and with different results. Making comparisons and judging the achievements of others and ourselves can lead to unhappiness and resistance. This resistance can deplete our energy levels and actually help us to under-achieve, rather than excel. We each have our own potential, so there is little point in comparing ourselves to others, or comparing one person to another. We can focus instead on finding our own true purpose to match our own potential.

Finding your true purpose
Once someone finds the things in life that are 'on purpose' for them, the things that really trigger their ambition, there comes a powerful flow of ready energy with which they can supply their drive. Something that absorbs people will allow them to go on way past normal human effort or endeavour. But finding what motivates us may require some patience on our part: it may be that the time is not yet come for us to harvest our ambitious energy, or there may be other aspects of the Universe that need to fall into place before our true purpose becomes obvious to us.

We may also need to let go of limiting beliefs about what is possible for us. Many people know what they would love to do, but don't attempt it because of all sorts of limiting beliefs. They may believe they *have* to stay where they are because of commitments, duty and habit or because maybe they wouldn't be good enough to make the grade. It certainly takes huge courage to go for it and turn dreams into reality, as there can be an element of risk involved in letting go of what is familiar in order to pursue our ambitions. Often, the gifts we receive when we commit to following our true purpose in life are in direct proportion to the size of the risk and the amount of trust we are prepared to invest in ourselves, other people and the Universe.

Following our true purpose can require a great deal of honesty. Our limiting beliefs about what is possible for us, as well as the way we have been influenced by other people in our lives, often make it quite difficult for us to be really honest about what really fires us up. Being totally honest with ourselves amongst all the distractions and agendas that our own egos and other people have around us can be very challenging . . .

Nurturing ambition and drive in yourself and other people

As we have seen, healthy ambition is a great source of energy and provides a means for us to progress in life, both individually and collectively. In order to nurture ambition we need to offer positive encouragement, yet without letting our own agenda interfere. For example, the parents of an ambitious child may start out by simply encouraging them, but then find themselves beginning to push the child for their own satisfaction. We also need to create space for ambition to be pursued without too many distractions, to give whatever support is needed (including supporting ourselves) and to strike a good balance so that other areas of life enhance the area of ambition.

Ambition and drive can be costly . . .

If ambition and drive is not focused, it can be quite costly in terms of energy. Too much ambition risks us losing our experience of life and people we are with now; if it is not handled with aware-ness, ambition can become an addiction. Ambition can become a blinkered habit; it can be a very effective way of avoiding looking at life. If we are unhealthily wrapped up in chasing particular goals we can lose our sense of perspective, lose loved ones, lose our health or lose life-balance in all sorts of ways.

If our ambition lacks direction, we may just keep going round in circles. One definition of insanity is to keep doing the same thing that isn't working: add ambitious energy to that and we really are barking mad. If our ambition becomes desperate and untethered, we may find ourselves using other people, taking advantage of them or being callous and unloving. Have you ever stepped on or used other people to fulfil your ambition? If you are ambitious, be careful not to sacrifice relationships or the fullness of life in order to fulfil your ambitions.

Things to do:

1. Think about some of the peak moments and achievements in your life. They don't have to be 'great' compared to the grand scheme of things, just the real peaks for you personally. Think about what you did to bring them about. Looking back, would it have possible for you to bring them about with less effort?
2. What really turns you on now? What would you love to be doing, or doing more of, that you would so easily be able to commit your energy to? Go ahead and do it. (Provided it's legal and doesn't offend anybody else!)
3. Think about your ambitions in relation to those close to you: are your ambitions really for them or for you? Support them in moving forwards in ways that they truly need, not in ways that you think they need. To know the difference between the two, ask them what would help them the most.
4. Whenever you are pursuing your ambition, notice if you are totally absorbed in it, or if you have negative feelings about whether you 'should' be doing it. For instance, do you feel that you 'should' be doing the housework or getting on with a project or paying the bills instead? You are here on earth for a few short years, so choose to do the things that will make the most valuable contribution and difference, and when you are doing them, commit yourself totally.
5. Commit yourself to following your ambition, but be aware of when you start 'pushing' and therefore creating possible resistance to good outcomes.
6. Channel energy into your ambitions: enjoy the ready supply that comes to you when you pursue your ambition.

DELEGATING AND MOTIVATING

To create success and win-win situations with other people and to channel ambition successfully, it is well worth becoming adept at delegating and motivating to others. No matter how self-sufficient we might be in life, we all rely on other people and need them to perform tasks for us in order to build successful lives for ourselves. Relying on someone else may entail something mundane like asking a family member to do something in the home or asking a colleague to do something in the workplace, or it may be a service such as getting the car fixed or booking a decent massage. It may mean getting someone to arrange a special blind date for us or asking someone to clinch a billion-dollar deal.

If we think about any aspect of life, it can be fun to reflect on just how many different people have helped us along the way. Something we take for granted, such as owning a car, relies on an almost infinite number of people to put us in the driving seat: there are the people who designed the car, who supplied the materials for it and who built it. Then there are the people who supplied the rubber for the tyres, the farmer who that looked after the cattle that supplied the leather for the seats and the people who built the car plant. There are the people who feed the car workers, the people who grow the food to supply the car-plant canteen, the transporters who carried the materials, the sales team that sold the car and the . . . oh well, this could go on for ever. The point is that we all rely on other people to a huge degree to do things for us.

This is why people whisperers understand the importance of asking other people for help in a way that works for all concerned, trusting in everyone's unique ability to play their part, and motivating all concerned with energy, balance and inspiration. What we are going to look at specifically now are people who do things for us that we have direct contact with: the people we delegate to and motivate in our daily lives.

Asking for help

We simply cannot do everything by ourselves: we will all have to ask others for help at some point in our lives. And so the best way to ask for help is to use very simple language in a way that can be easily understood, without 'loading' the way we ask with a negative emotional charge. That sounds like quite a challenge and yet beautifully simple at the same time.

There is great value in asking directly and openly for help or advice when we need it: the worst thing the other person can say is 'No'. Ideally, we ask for help from a place of detachment, in which we are clear about what we want and in which our emotional state will not be affected, regardless of whether or not the other person complies with our request. Asking for something with a negative emotional charge means that there is anger, frustration, hidden force, control and over-use of power, apology, desperation, hope or any other kind of unhelpful energy in our voice, the words we use, our energy and body language.

If we feel anger or tension when we ask for help or delegate a task to someone, even if we attempt to hide it, the other party will feel it. This means that even if they respond to what we have asked, their carrying out of the task will be tainted by that negative emotion. It is very easy to introduce resentment into a situation when delegating and, unfortunately, it can be equally hard to remove the feeling once it is there. If we load a request with negative emotion, it is almost bound to bring up a negative emotion in the other person in response, which is why asking with detachment is such a useful skill.

Building relationships

In order to achieve the best response when motivating others or delegating to them, take the time to build rapport first. Imagine making a 'delegation sandwich', in which the request is the filling, and relationship/rapport is the bread wrapped around that request, so that the person receiving the request gets a bite of rapport with every mouthful: before, during and after the task! If you are going to delegate tasks or responsibility to someone, think about the ways that other people have delegated things to you in the past: how did they achieve this most effectively? Think as well about the ways in which people may have really put your back up when they delegated something to you or made you feel resentful when you did what they asked. Be sure to round off any delegation by revisiting your rapport and relationship with the other person after the task is completed: it will certainly be worth while.

When delegating, it sometimes helps to smooth things along if we give a simple reason about why we need to have something done and we let it be known that we will be appreciative. However, it is best to avoid going into long, apologetic explanations, as these will weaken our position and may make us sound uncertain as to whether our request is reasonable. If someone understands the reason for or value of doing something, they are more likely to be happy to do it. To get someone to perform a difficult task, we can create some initial movement by getting the other person to work with us; then once we are working together, we can guide them around to the more difficult agenda.

Remember that it is entirely the free choice of the other person as to whether they do what we ask or not; by and large we cannot make them. Even if they are an employee of ours, they can still choose not to do what is asked of them; although it is up to them to handle the consequences of that choice, of course.

Ask and let go

Once we have delegated something to someone and they have understood our request, we need to be sure to give them the room to carry it out without 'getting in the way'.' Some people react very badly to being pushed or forced to do something, so it is best to *ask* them rather than *tell* them what we want. Even better, we could set things up so that they offer to do the task from their own initiative. See if you can ask someone to do something when it would be easy for them to respond: choose a good time when they are in just the right place or state to do what you asked of them.

It can be very challenging to stand back and allow someone else to get on without our interfering if the delegated task in question is important to us, or if we live by the maxim '*If you want something done properly, do it yourself*'. But, if motivated in the right way, most people will do the best they can do in the circumstances . . . anyway, we just have to trust that that is what they are doing and stop interfering!

Once we have delegated something, it requires a certain amount of inner strength on our part to allow the possibility of mistakes being made. That can be pretty difficult, especially if a $10 million contract rests upon it. But then, if the task in hand is that important and we really don't trust anyone else to do it, perhaps we would be better off doing it ourselves in the first place, and not delegating at all. That way, if we blow the $10 million contract, we will only have to forgive ourselves!

Handling mistakes

If we feel confident about delegating and giving others the room to get on with the task in hand, the next challenge involves not punishing them for their mistakes. Generally speaking, people aren't stupid (if you are delegating important stuff to people you think are stupid, perhaps you need to ask a few questions about yourself!), and they will usually realise when they have made a mistake and will look to avoid repeating it. If we are able to acknowledge mistakes and their consequences without punishing the perpetrator, or coming across as judgemental or accusing, we will be offering that person a huge opportunity to grow – a spiritual gift if you like. It may be useful to explore what went wrong by discussing together what has been learned from the outcome (mistake). Or it might be worth asking, 'What could we do differently next time?'

We have to remind ourselves as many times as necessary that fear of making mistakes cripples progress for all of us. The best place to start learning to handle other people's mistakes is to learn to handle our own mistakes. Forgiving ourselves, especially if we are driven people or perfectionists, can be quite a challenging leap. Ask yourself: what do I need to risk? What is the worst thing can happen if I get it wrong?

Motivation

When we are delegating or motivating to someone else, we need to find a way of meeting the other person's agenda as well as our own: that way, motivation becomes 'self-motivation'. What is more, if we can lead and motivate people by winning their hearts, then their minds and bodies normally follow!

Ask yourself:

- What are the things in life that motivate you to such an extent that it is no effort whatsoever to do them? What is special about the things that motivate you compared to the stuff you are not interested in?
- If you want to motivate other people, do you know what motivates them naturally? What is in it for them?
- In what areas of activity in these people's lives do they come alive? What kind of things are they doing when they are most self-motivated: creating, being technical, solving problems, interacting with people etc.?
- What would have to change for them to feel more motivated in areas of their lives where it is a bit of an effort? What else could they be gaining from those activities?
- How can you match what you want from them with what they want for themselves?

Motivating others by valuing, praising and rewarding them, say financially or with affection, depending on the circumstances, is all very well and goes a long way. However, the most powerful way to motivate someone lies in helping that person to find interest and delight in the actual *doing* of the task itself – so that the very *doing* of it is its own reward. This is far more direct than rewarding someone after the event: when the act of doing brings them joy, absorption or pleasure, their motivation comes from an infinite source because they are connected with 'being'. When someone is doing whatever is right for that person, they will be effortlessly motivated.

When we are doing something that motivates us to such an extent that it takes no apparent effort on our part, we may have entered a state of mind in which we lose track of time and become present-moment focused. When we are fully in the present and absorbed in whatever we are doing, motivation is almost a redundant concept: no motivation is required, because in this state things just get along by themselves.

Ask yourself:

- Have you or do you enter that state of being totally absorbed in something in the present moment? What things can get you into that state? What is it about those activities that makes you do that?

◆ Can you find any of those qualities in things you do that are not so easy for you?

Nurturing talents

By motivating others and helping them to find their true potential, we may be giving them a very valuable gift, but we are also bringing a gift into the situation for ourselves too. Motivating people to expand themselves is a two-way street: as they expand into their talents, we share that expansion with them. Lastly, remember that, somehow, by nurturing our own talents and abilities, so that we become as great as we can be, we allow others to expand by following our example.

Things to do:

1. Practise delegating without emotion. Detach yourself from the response you receive. You never know what the response to your request will be until you have communicated it.
2. Practise making requests in different ways, until you find the key to each particular person.
3. Find ways to match your agenda with the other person's: that way, motivation becomes a joint effort and 1+1=3. Wow!
4. Look for ways to motivate and enable people in your relationships to become more of who they are. Show the way by being motivated towards growing in yourself.

The Power of Questions

One of the most powerful tools for creating success in life is our ability to ask good questions. It is undoubtedly those people in history who asked great questions who have helped the human race to move forwards the most. The quality of the questions we ask creates the life we want to live: everything starts with a question, so if we ask a great question, we stand far more chance of creating something great than if we ask a poor question.

Question Yourself!

You have probably noticed by now that this book has lots of questions for you to answer: that's because there is only one person in the Universe who has all the answers you need, and that is YOU. Asking yourself the questions in this book *and answering them* will almost certainly move you forwards, so be caring towards yourself and answer them. Don't just read the questions and skip over them. You'll be amazed at what you find out about your life, loves, relationships and yourself: from yourself!

The people whisperer knows that the power and the gift of asking good questions is a part of creating and exploring life and relationships. The right question always leads to the right answer.

Asking People Questions

Asking the right questions can open up huge possibilities for us in our interactions with people in all sorts of circumstances. By asking people questions in a genuine way, we let them know that we are genuinely interested in them. People can find this irresistible, delightful or, because they are not used to someone showing them this level of interest, they may feel uncomfortable and shy. This can be a great way to let them know that we are interested in them and we are engaging with them. Asking genuine questions and waiting for the answer by truly listening is a way of showing love to a fellow human.

Asking questions can bring about incredible answers and asking questions for outside help or input is often a huge benefit: remember other people's perception is different to our own and this can be an advantage or a disadvantage. Sometimes asking the right question at the right time will enable someone to find an answer they didn't even know consciously themselves before the answer came out of them.

Asking Yourself Questions

Asking ourselves the right questions can lead us to all the information and keys we need to create the life we would like. By asking ourselves questions that we don't think we know the answers to, we start to use our all-knowing unconscious mind. The unconscious mind is our mainframe computer, storing everything that has ever happened to us, even the events that we don't think we can remember. It is also connected to the master mainframe computer, the Universe, and when asked the right question it can sometimes come up with staggering answers, the like of which we could never have known on our own. Try it. Remember that questions raised at this kind of level are not usually answered in words or thoughts made up of words; the answers normally appear in life somehow, and they appear in their own time too!

We can take this one stage further, by not only asking ourselves and other people questions, but also directly asking questions of the Universe, the Source or whatever we want to call it. There is nothing to lose. Putting questions out there is the same as putting any other word, thought or action out there: they will be answered in some way. Ask a question and an answer will come back . . . although not, perhaps, in the form you might have expected it!

Ways to Ask Brilliant Questions . . .

The whole point of asking questions is to facilitate an answer, so it is important that questions are asked in a way that makes them easy to answer. Here are some ways to ask brilliant questions . . .

1. Always ask questions of others or of yourself that frame things positively, e.g. 'What can we do to get along better together?', rather than 'What do we do that makes us keep falling out all the time?'
2. Ask questions that begin with words 'which', 'how', 'when', 'where' etc., but avoid using the word 'why'. Now you're wondering 'why' it is a word to avoid aren't you? The word

'why' can imply a judgement, and therefore makes the person who is asked more defensive: in effect the word 'why' can make it harder for the person to answer the question, since unconsciously they are expecting to be judged:

Why did you stay late at work with your secretary?'

Why did you say I was a selfish lover in front of my mates?'

Why did you nick those apples from next door's tree?'

Why did you sink all our savings into that crashed investment company?'

3. Ask questions that come from the heart of you, not just from your head.

4. Make your questions easy to understand, so that the other person can focus on their answer, not on what the hell the questions meant.

5. Ask questions without emotion in your voice. Otherwise, it would be easy for the other person to hear the emotion more than the question.

6. Remember that you may think you know the answer to the question you are asking, but the answer you have in mind may not be the right answer for the other person: everyone has their own answers to life's questions.

7. Ask the right question and the answer will appear. There is a Buddhist idea that the answer is always contained within the question: well it is, but it does require exactly the right question to be asked!

8. When you ask someone a question, wait for the answer and listen to it. Hold the space: immerse yourself in quiet and pay full attention to the person who is answering.

9. Avoid questions that make the person answering feel blamed or accused of being wrong or 'bad'.

Things to do:

1. Try this experiment for finding something lost or mislaid, such as your car keys: think specifically about what you want to find and ask yourself when you had them last. Then ask yourself 'Where did I put it,' or 'What did I do with it last?' Completely avoid saying or thinking anything negative along the lines of 'I have lost it' or 'I don't know

where it is' etc. Relax and let the answer come to you: you may find yourself simply going over to the object you lost without even thinking about it. Your unconscious knows all the answers; you simply have to ask the question in a way that it can answer. Now use the same technique to manifest answers to other questions in your life.

2. Start noticing the kind of questions you ask yourself on a daily basis, about your work, your relationships and your life in general. Think about reframing questions so that you get more favourable answers.

3. Ask other people questions in ways that help them to express themselves more constructively when they are around you.

4. Realise that questions are a huge power behind creating your experiences and the quality of all that happens to you. Use the power of questions to create whatever you want . . . no one would have invented the light bulb, the combustion engine, the wheel or the condom if they hadn't asked a few questions first!

Now we have looked at some ways to work with others to create success for all involved, the time has come to look at expressing our own personal power in Secret Eleven.

Secret Eleven

Express Your Personal Power

Personal Power

Much of this book is about personal power. By nurturing our personal power we improve our abilities to communicate effectively, to make a difference, to be of value and to inspire others. Stepping into our personal power means learning to trust that what we want will come to us, that we are attractive when we are our true selves. It means getting to know ourselves and others, and being able to experience a life filled with love and joy (and also to laugh at the whole thing!). This is why successful people whisperers do not shy away from stepping into the immense personal power that is possessed by each one of us. Whilst they also have great modesty, they have true presence, self-reliance and inner strength, and are incredibly inspiring to others.

What is 'Personal Power?'

True personal power is made up of many elements and is created by different people in different ways, according to their individual personalities. If we step into our own personal power, we will have a sense of inner security and strength that comes from being centred and we will be more likely to follow our own path and be true to ourselves. As a result, others will be touched by our lives and may be inspired to follow our example; thus, by stepping into our own personal power, we enable others to grow in their own personal power too.

Personal power has nothing to do with exercising command over other people: if anything, it is about having a high level of command over ourselves. True personal power is 'of the light', which means that there is no need to dominate others. It is totally secure, in and of itself, which is why people find it so attractive, because it seeks nothing from anyone else. Everyone has their own realm of personal power. It is an internal quality and therefore we cannot look to anyone else to give us permission to claim it for ourselves. So allow yourself to be brilliant and beautiful: it is your birthright.

Inner strength

It takes inner strength to live fully in society. Our modern, people-filled world can be a mentally and emotionally harsh place. Having inner strength means we can cope more easily with the challenges of human life, follow our own path and still be true to ourselves. Inner strength means being who we are and living as we wish to, without allowing others to throw us about, to rock us emotionally or divert us from our course. We remain flexible, aware of our internal and external worlds, responsive, empathic and compassionate to others and responsible for our own actions.

True inner strength enables us to show our vulnerability and feel comfortable enough to appear weak, because we don't need to pretend or present a tough front to others. People are often drawn to this kind of expression of personal power because they know it is totally honest, that we are not attempting to fool any of the people any of the time – and that begins by not fooling ourselves! Yet, we also need to remember that however well we conduct ourselves, some people may react against someone who has high levels of personal power and integrity, because it can challenge their own model of who they are.

Self-reliance

Our personal power is increased by our being self-reliant, which means being able to cope with whatever comes our way, and supplying ourselves with the energy, resources, love and approval we need without being 'needy' of other people. When we are self-reliant we can handle life because we trust ourselves and the

165

Universe. We know that all things are temporary: nothing lasts for ever, whether it is a good time, a bad time, an ecstatic time or a totally and utterly impossible time. Whatever is happening and whatever other people are doing around us or to us, when we are self-reliant we keep our own peace; we listen and stay in touch with our bodies and remain centred, even amidst chaos. Being self-reliant means we decide how we feel. We respond instead of reacting and are quietly loving of others, even in difficult circumstances. We are flexible and able to change what we are doing in order to respond to a person or situation appropriately, bringing in fresh ideas and new ways of looking at things.

Being self-reliant does not mean that we don't interact with other people or form meaningful bonds. Quite the opposite – because we do not need to feed off other people, we are more able to engage in healthy and mutually beneficial relationships, rather than seeking approval from others. Self-reliant people do not have need to take centre stage, be the main focus of attention or do most of the talking: they are comfortable with who they are, without needing public support or reinforcement of their worth.

Being Self-Reliant

To be self-reliant, avoid weakening yourself in relation to other people by doing any of the following:

- attempting to impress
- trying to justify yourself
- looking for compliments or approval
- expressing too much non-genuine attention to someone
- gossiping or making small-talk to *try* and connect with someone
- trying to win favour
- pretending to be interested in someone else's every word

Personal presence

Personal presence is a very nebulous and difficult thing to rationalise or arrange by formula: like other aspects of personal power, it is can be made up of many different factors. Although presence is largely experienced by other people as an outward quality, it is really a reflection of internal qualities. A person with true presence has a sense of self-worth and self-belief; they know their life purpose has value and that they are here to make a difference in the world. When they speak, it is because they have something they believe is important or worth while to say. Someone with personal presence moves and uses their body in a centred and purposeful way. Their body and their energy communicate outwards and touch people and, at the same time, they hold their own space with quiet confidence. Someone with personal presence brings an 'energy' with them that we can almost touch: this energy comes from their sense of who they are and their focused awareness of their purpose in life.

To reveal your personal presence, let your light shine out into the world: but be aware that it is not always appropriate to have our levels of personal presence turned up to the max in every situation. Some people may find a high degree of personal presence a little too bright and may even shrink away from us, unless they are wearing their shades! As you become aware of the power of your personal presence and its effect on other people, experiment with toning it up or down, depending on whom you are with and what you want to achieve.

Being Inspiring

One noticeable quality of people who have stepped into their personal power is that they are inspiring. People who are inspiring have a vision that they believe in, and that others can see and believe in too; they possess a quality that touches something in other people, enabling them to release their own energy, creativity and action too. An inspiring person sets an example of greatness and enthusiastic energy that helps people to see their own unrealised potential. Having seen that projection of themselves in someone they admire, they are set free from their limitations and spurred on to expand in their own way.

Ask yourself:

◆ How do you inspire other people?
◆ Who inspires you and how do they do that?

Someone who is inspiring gives the very real impression that they are stretching themselves to achieve and be the best they can be; they excel at being who they are and communicate an enthusiasm that is almost contagious, making others want to be more like them in some way.

Modesty and Humility

The aspects of personal power discussed so far are potentially very powerful tools for people whisperers to have in their kitbags. That is why it is important to balance such tools as inner strength, self-reliance and personal presence with modesty and humility. Interestingly, there is great power in these qualities too, when they come from a place of integrity. Being modest and humble can help to keep us grounded, especially when we have been exchanging energy at the high altitudes involved when we are in our personal power. Modesty and humility also prevent us from believing all of our own press about our personal power and presence! Remember that all of the qualities discussed in this Secret are coming from the right place; they are not born out of arrogance or a need for attention and the approval of others.

Things to do:

1. Don't be shy: dare to step into your personal power and be as magnificent as you can be. Remember that all people are equals underneath, which means you have as much potential for personal power as anyone else on the planet. That *is* an exciting and scary thought.
2. Look at ways in which people around you, either at home or at work, may try to make you less self-reliant than you could be. Trust yourself to know that, whatever happens, you can cope.

3. Develop a sense of presence: check in with your internal energy levels and sense of purpose. Allow your light to shine out into the world.

4. Remain grounded: remember that you need to be able to walk with your feet on the earth whilst you're still alive. Let modesty and humility keep you grounded and powerful at the same time.

Attraction

We have seen how people whisperers enjoy high degrees of self-reliance and personal power; consequently they do not rely on approval from others in order to feel attractive or needed. They know that if they feel totally comfortable within themselves they will attract all they need into their lives.

What Does Being Attractive Mean?

Being attractive involves far more than just the way we look. Being truly attractive means that people want to share our time and company; it can mean more clients want to do business with us; or it might mean friends want to walk that extra mile for us. True attractiveness can mean that people are drawn to us with a loving feeling; it can mean people want to rip our clothes off and make mad passionate love with us – in fact being 'attractive' can mean so many things and opens up a wide range of possibilities.

It is easy to assume that being attractive is purely a matter of physical appearance and looks, but it isn't (thankfully!). When we first see someone, there are a number of other elements of attraction involved aside from that person's appearance. In addition to the way someone 'looks', their body and its surrounding energy will be continually projecting that person's thoughts, emotions and intentions out into the world. And, although we may not consciously notice what the person's true self is projecting in this way, the signals they send out will nevertheless reach our unconscious and make that person more or less attractive to us, regardless of physical beauty.

Ask yourself:

- What makes one person attractive to you and another person not attractive to you?
- What is it about some people that seems to make everyone find them attractive?
- And other people that few other people seem to find attractive?
- And more pressingly – how can we make ourselves more attractive to everybody?!!!

The illusion of physical looks

What we see when we look in the mirror is not what everyone else sees: what we are seeing is our own interpretation of how we look. When we look at someone else, we often make automatic assessments, comparisons and judgements, however inaccurate, about what kind of person they are and therefore how attractive that person is to us. For example:

- He's got long hair, he must be a lazy hippy.[1]
- She's wearing scruffy clothes, she must be a drop-out.[2]
- He's got a shaved head, he must be a hooligan.[3]
- She's wearing a nun's habit, she must be very devout and pious.[4]

(see below for the truth!)

Can we make other people find us more attractive?

We cannot make other people find us attractive any more than we can make them like a particular food. Moreover, if we rely on other people to decide whether we are attractive or not, we make ourselves 'victims' of their opinions. So instead of trying to change ourselves or saying we *should be* different to how we are

[1] He is a famous actor who has grown his hair for a part in a lavish production of *Macbeth* for the Royal Shakespeare Company.

[2] She is the chief executive of a major PLC corporation on her way to help out at a local homeless charity, as she does every Saturday morning.

[3] He has been receiving chemotherapy.

[4] She is a call girl on her way home after seeing a gentleman with a taste for a particular habit!

already, first let's take an honest look at how attractive we are right now . . .

Ask yourself:

- How much do you need to be 'liked'?
- Can you feel happy with your own company?
- What messages does your body convey to others? What does the way you stand, sit and walk say about you? What does the speed at which and the way in which you move say about you?
- How do you feel inside about yourself?
- What thoughts and emotions drive you through life?
- What feelings do you wear on your face? What feelings do you attempt to hide behind your face?
- What kind of 'energy' surrounds you? What atmosphere do you bring with you when you enter a room or situation?
- What qualities do you already have that are attractive?
- How much do you rely on other people's opinions in order to feel attractive?
- What does the way you dress, your hair and make-up say or hide about you?
- Who are the most attractive people in your life? What makes these people attractive?
- Do you see any of those qualities in yourself? What could you do to increase these qualities in yourself?

Inner Self-confidence

Probably the most universally attractive quality is inner self-confidence, but this doesn't mean we have to become egotistical or think we are better than anyone else. 'Inner' self-confident people are comfortable in their own skin: they have an inner peace and are accepting of themselves and others, which gives them a stillness that is attractive. By way of contrast, 'outwardly' self-confident people rely on approval from other people or outside events in order to feel good about themselves: consequently their self-confidence is a front, they are all huff and puff – 'Aren't I marvellous', 'See how the ground loves me to walk on it', etc. This front is normally an attempt to hide their insecurity, but it can make them uncomfortable company to be with.

If you don't have any inner self-confidence, how do you find it? As you follow the secrets contained within this book, answering the questions and following the 'Things to do', you will be getting to know your true self and becoming more comfortable about your place in the world: this alone is the best nourishment to feed your inner self-confidence. As your self-knowledge grows, in time you may be taken aback by how highly regarded you are by others and by how so many people want to share your presence. The more at peace you are within yourself, the more people, cats, dogs, horses, good fortune, opportunities and everything else the Universe has to offer will be attracted to you.

You can't please all the people all the time!

We have been exploring how to become more attractive to more people, but we may not be successful with everyone . . . Well, tough, there's nothing we can do to control the people who are missing out on our delightful presence in their lives! Let them live with it, let them go, while we happily get on with being our true selves and enjoying our own lives. We can take back our own power by deciding for ourselves that we are attractive, whatever they may think.

Things to do:

1. Start noticing how special you are: look at all the things you can do that you normally take for granted. Something that seems relatively small and insignificant to you, like cooking or solving a crossword, may be a huge achievement in someone else's eyes.
2. Smile a lot and dress for *you*.
3. Take steps to help build more inner self-confidence: remember self-confidence comes from being kind to yourself and nurturing a sense of inner peace within. Look at the section in Secret Two 'Eaves-dropping in on your thoughts' and see what inner people whispering you do that makes you feel more or less attractive. Give yourself a break!

4. Shift your focus away from simply how you look on the outside: everyone looks the same on the inside anyway (roughly speaking)!
5. Drop expectations of other people and drop the need for others to approve of you.

TRUST

There are many benefits to nurturing our personal power, our sense of innate attractiveness and our self-reliance: one of those benefits is the increased ability to trust in whatever life has to offer us. People whisperers know the value of trusting: trusting themselves, trusting comrades and loved ones, trusting professionals, trusting outcomes and trusting the processes of life. Every time we get in an aeroplane we trust the pilot; every time we go to the doctors we trust them. Every time we eat in a restaurant we trust the chef, every time we drive a car we trust the other road users, and every time we fall completely in love we trust our lovers. Our whole lives are built on trust and yet when we are required to consciously trust others with our hearts, loved ones, homes or business deals, we often find it hard.

This does not mean that people whisperers never expect to be let down; rather, they accept that people change, that nothing in life is for certain and all things are fluid, including trust.

Have you ever trusted someone and been let down?

If that hasn't happened to you then you are quite a rarity. Most of us have surely experienced trusting someone and being let down. This is one of life's fundamental lessons and one which gives us a choice: we can close down and shrink away from trusting people in the future, or we can use the experience to open further to life.

How can we ever know for sure that someone can be really trusted? We can't: we just have to trust them! If we absolutely knew that someone could be trusted, perhaps it wouldn't be 'trust', it would be a certainty . . . 'Trust' has an element of uncertainty about it: there is the possibility, however remote it may be, that the trust may be broken. Perhaps that is what makes trust such a valuable and precious commodity – because it is possible to break it.

Ask yourself:

◆ Who can you really trust? Can you really trust your friends, the government, employer, employees, business partner, kids, husband, wife, your husband or wife with your best friend!

◆ Here's an interesting question . . . can you trust yourself? Can you trust yourself to be worthy of your dreams, to be faithful to your own values, to be yourself and do what is right for you, to not let yourself down when it matters, to stand up for yourself, your principles or your loved ones if the chips are down?

It is fair to say that trust can take a long time to build up and only a moment to destroy. But by refusing to trust anyone else in the future, we will keep ourselves in a place where we continue to be hurt by that moment in the past when we were let down. If we spend our lives believing we cannot trust, we are likely to create a life in which our trust is repeatedly broken.

Can other people trust you?

Hopefully your answer to the question above is 'yes' (but you are free to change your mind and appear not trustworthy!). However, there may be times in all of our lives when, even though we are essentially trustworthy people, being true to ourselves requires us to do something that runs contrary to another person's trust in us. This is because our beliefs and values may change during our lifetimes, which means that where we could once be 'trusted' to *be* or *do* a certain thing, when our beliefs change we can no longer be 'trusted' for things that we previously were.

Trusting the Right People

Here are some simple steps we can take to help us to know if we are trusting the right people:

- ◆ Check with your inner self: how do you feel about this person? What are your emotions telling you about them?
- ◆ Use your intuition: what are your hunches telling you?
- ◆ Listen to your body: do you feel relaxed or uncomfortable?

Trusting 'The Process'

Trusting the process means accepting the way people and situations are, and letting things develop and unfold as they are meant to without interference on our part. It can be a real challenge of trust for us to set things in motion and then let them happen, allowing them to run their course. What we need comes to us, but we don't always know why people are doing what they're doing or why things are apparently more difficult than we think they *should be*. It is only when we look back (or see things from a higher perspective) that we can see the benefit or purpose of why processes happen in a particular way on our life's journey.

Trusting is about learning to trust the process and allowing it to lead to the right outcome. If we ever find ourselves *trying* to steer people or events by pushing, cajoling and manipulating them to get a certain end result, or obsessively hoping things will turn out a certain way, we aren't trusting that things will turn out for the best. And by not trusting in the outcome we interfere with the flow of the processes involved and limit the space available for things to turn out in the most natural way.

If we trust people to play their part, yes, sometimes we may be let down or disappointed that they didn't do things exactly how we wanted or expected them to do. But if we learn to trust the process, we can be sure that the right outcomes will always find their way to us – perhaps in forms that are different or better than those we expected.

Trusting the Universe

Against all odds, we survive by living on the thin outer crust of a piece of mostly molten rock that spins constantly at about a thousand miles per hour, flying through space at heaven-knows what speed, exposed to all kinds of physical threats, bugs, viruses, accidents, violence, meteorites, B movies, spam-mail and harsh environments – *but we are still here*. So how can we not trust the Universe?

People who trust the Universe don't just sit back and become sofa vegetables: they are still active in the world, but they have a sense of being supported in it. They allow themselves to be in communication with the incredible, infinitely complex happening that is the Universe and they flow with it. Have a think about it: if you trusted the Universe to take care of you, to bring you the people you needed, to keep you safe, to supply you with your survival needs, to give you amazing experiences and learning opportunities, how much pressure would that take off you?

The next time you feel you have too much responsibility; that you can't cope and things are running away with you; that you don't know how you're going to manage, you need more help, see if trusting the Universe helps. Hand things over, trust in the power that created the Big Bang and put us here in the first place: remember that power has infinite resources, which is even more than the USA has!

Things to do:

1. In what ways can you or can't you trust yourself? For example, can you trust yourself to be honest when it counts, to acknowledge other people's feelings or to do your personal best at all times? Most of all, can you be trusted to be true to yourself?
2. How much can other people trust you? Are you reliable at work and dependable at home? Do you keep your word? When you appear trustworthy as far as other people are concerned, are you always being true to yourself?
3. Next time you are under pressure, why not trust that the Universe will work things out? See if it makes you feel more comfortable, and whether any solutions appear that you hadn't thought of.

HOLDING THE INTENTION (AND SOFTENING AROUND THE RESISTANCE)

Having considered how our ability to trust comes from a sense of inner personal power, let's take this concept to a higher level by seeing how trust works when combined with intention. Successful people whisperers know the value of allowing their intentions to manifest themselves by giving them space in which to unfold. They allow people to play their part in the process without using force of will to control events: it is simply a matter of asking for what they want and trusting the flow.

Firstly, we need to know what outcome we want. Many of us avoid choosing or naming what we would like to happen to us for various reasons that are usually to do with our limiting beliefs. The truth is, if we believe something is possible and we believe that we deserve it, then it can happen for us. Here's the reality: anything is possible and, as a divine being, you deserve whatever you wish for – who ever told you otherwise?

Pushing and *trying* too hard

Once we know what our goal or outcome is, we humans normally start pushing, hassling or towsing like a dog with a toy rabbit to take control and make it happen. We think that this is the way to overcome any resistance that is present, whether that resistance comes from within ourselves (very common), or whether we think it comes from another person or the Universe. But what we perceive as resistance is not resistance at all: it is feedback, which means we need to ask ourselves what it is telling us.

We may need to invest energy, work and focus into what we want, but *trying* too hard with anything or anyone is actually very uneconomical and ineffective, creating resistance. Someone or something else can only offer resistance to us if we give them something to push against; but if we soften, they no longer have anything to resist.

Here's how to avoid trying too hard:

◆ If you find yourself becoming involved in this proactive *trying* process and pushing through any resistance, pause, take a breath, step back and soften in your body and mind about the whole thing. Let the tension drop from it and allow it to *be*.

◆ If you soften in this way around other people they will have an unconscious sense of relief, you will appear more attractive to them and they will have the space to give you more of what you want.

◆ If you soften in this way around the Universe, amazing things will start to come up for you; people will think you are plain lucky and life will expand beyond anything you imagined possible.

Softening Around Other People

If someone isn't doing what we want them to do, taking a longer time or going a different route to the one we had anticipated, it is best to avoid pushing them, getting impatient or interfering with them. The chances are that they are going the right way for them at the right speed for them. This doesn't mean we won't achieve our own final desired outcome; in fact we have more chance of achieving it if we soften around the resistance coming from the other party and allow our intention to manifest itself for us regardless. That said, the more something or someone means to us, the more challenging it can be to soften around the resistance.

If we openly fight with someone in order to reach the outcome we want, we are investing our energy and focus in the fight, not in our intention. And so, even if we realise our intention after fighting the resistance, the outcome will not have the same easy quality about it as it would if we had held on to the intention and softened around it.

Of course we can disagree with someone over a principle, idea or behaviour, but if we do it without an emotional charge attached, then it will not cost us so much and will not give someone else anything to push against: it would be like they have been pushing against thin air.

Softening around resistance has nothing to do with 'giving up' our goals, but it does have everything to do with giving up wasting energy and getting in the way. We have to be quite in touch with ourselves and very vigilant to avoid indulging in the very human habits of pushing, trying or fighting to make something we want come about. *This is not the same as giving up!* Quite the opposite: because we are holding our intention and softening, our energy is quietly powerful and the Universe or other people have plenty of space in which to find ways to deliver our intention to us. Often our intention comes in a way we have not expected when we use this tool, often much better and much easier . . . People around us may call it luck . . . hmmm, who knows?

Things to do:

1. Notice what you have been doing when things happen really easily for you. More than that, notice not what you do, but how you are *being* when things happen really easily for you.
2. Notice things that you obsess about, that you can't let go of and can't stop thinking about over and over. How ineffective is this and how much energy does it cost you?
3. Notice what your body is doing when resistance is present: see if you can let the resistance out of your body, by relaxing your shoulders, back or wherever else you habitually hold the resistance in you.
4. Drop the need to press or control others: remind yourself that none of this will matter to you in a hundred years' time.

Stepping into your personal power means expressing your birthright as a human being, which is even greater than you might suppose. In the final secret, we will discover how our human 'being' is intertwined with the infinite magnificence of the Universe itself.

Secret Twelve

The Universe Gives You What You Ask For

People whisperers know that true communication entails communicating not only with themselves, and with other people, but also with the Universe at large. This is one of the highest levels of awareness, and it means understanding that every communication is heard by the Universe and responded to in some way. People whisperers are therefore conscious of the kind of life and relationships they are creating at any given moment through the messages that they send out into the world.

Even when we don't intend to, we ask the Universe for things. And we may accidentally ask the Universe to give to us the very things we wouldn't intentionally want in a million years. When it seems that fate is slinging a dreadful hand at us, it can be difficult to accept that we may actually have asked, intentionally or not, for whatever is happening in our lives. Never have truer words been said than those in the old adage, 'Be careful what you ask for: you might get it!'

However, there is another, more positive, side to the coin: if we are responsible for asking for the experiences, life and relationships that we get in our lives, it means that we are in the driving seat. All we need to do is to communicate – whisper what we want – in such a way as to create the life we want to live. Wow! Anything is possible.

HOW TO ASK FOR WHAT YOU WANT IN A WAY THAT WORKS

◆ Provided you ask in a clear way, the Universe will instantly start to set things in motion to answer your call, whether you are aware of it or not.

◆ Become aware of how you communicate with yourself, other people and the Universe through your thoughts, words, emotions and actions. Start to see how these factors create and contribute to the situation you are in now.

◆ Ask for what you want in a quiet and unattached way. Put your request out there, stay out of the way and allow it to be answered. Resist the temptation to hassle and chafe about it: you have sent the message, so let go. You wouldn't post a letter and keep hold of a piece of thread attached to it whilst it makes its way through the mail system, would you? If you did, it would never get to its destination. If you keep a hold on the things you ask for in life, they will not be responded to because they will never really 'get there'.

◆ Recognise when your asking is being answered, even in small ways. Sometimes the universe will communicate back to you by giving you a small sample of what you asked for, as if it is saying 'Is this what you mean?' If you show appreciation for any sign of your wish being fulfilled, even if in a small way, the Universe will be clearer about what you want and give you more of the same. Remember that everything in life is a stepping stone, another step along the way: there is no actual end, just more doorways to go through and more new territory to explore.

◆ Sometimes the Universe hears what we ask for and replies by apparently giving us something different to what we think we asked for. This is because, although we may have attempted to communicate something specific through words, our higher selves simultaneously communicate our true needs or values at a more profound level. The Universe gives us something to fulfil or meet that deeper need, often in ways that are far more suitable for us than the thing we thought we wanted. For example, we may ask for a flashy sports car and, although we don't get the car, shortly afterwards we meet a wonderful new lover. It transpires that the request for the car was just our limited way of thinking that we might improve our chances of attracting some love interest if we owned a flash motor. Happily, the Universe heard the real request – our deep desire to attract an exciting lover – and knew the car was unnecessary. Think about what underlying values or needs you want to fulfil when you make any requests of the Universe. Then allow it to answer in the way it knows to be for your highest good. Be aware that higher values, based on loving or generous acts, are often more easily manifested. You will not be disappointed.

◆ Phrase things in the positive: avoid using words like 'don't', 'can't' and 'not' as in 'what I *don't* want is to be lonely in old age', or 'I just *can't* ever see me finding my true love, my true soul mate' or ' I am *not* going to find it easy to get another worthwhile job'. The difficulty with this is that the Universe will hear you and do its best to make sure you are proved right: so you are pretty likely to end up lonely in old age, not find your true love and not get a worthwhile job.

◆ Drop limiting beliefs. This means letting go of the thoughts you have about what is not possible for you in life. Those thoughts hold you back. How do you really know what is possible and what isn't?

◆ Notice in what ways you may be communicating to the Universe – through what you say, think or do – that may not bring what you want: or, even worse, what you say, think or do that may bring you stuff that you definitely don't want! What do you communicate to the Universe that attracts the sort of relationships, whether they are personal or work-related, that don't work for you? 'Ask and ye shall receive' . . . Yikes!

◆ The Universe will bring you the right people you need to fulfil any request you put in. When these people arrive, all you have to do is to recognise them and use your people whispering skills to integrate them into your life in a way that works for them and for you . . . and, yes, that may be the tricky part!

◆ There's no need to SHOUT! You can whisper almost at the volume level of utter silence and the Universe will hear you, provided the request you communicate is clear and congruent.

Things to do:

1. Think of everything that has ever happened to you and all that is happening to you as though you had asked for it all. (OK, you may have been mad, but that's not up for discussion here!)
2. If you have asked for everything that has happened to you, even the bits where you felt like a mushroom (that means being kept in the dark and having dung thrown on you), ask yourself what you may have wanted each event to teach you. What did you potentially stand to benefit from it? If you can do this, you will be in a far more powerful and responsible place as a result.
3. Look at some of the people around you and see how they 'ask' for what happens to them.
4. Experiment with 'whispering' a wish or thought incredibly clearly and quietly, then let go of it. See what happens.
5. Practise 'asking' for the relationships and life you want by doing more of what works and less of what doesn't. This may sound ridiculously obvious, but because of our attachments, patterns, habits and beliefs, this can be a bizarrely difficult thing to actually do!
6. Experiment with thinking thoughts to the Universe that request the life, relationships and experiences that you would really like: be bold and ambitious . . . To reiterate, ANYTHING IS POSSIBLE!

CHOOSING YOUR LIFE'S COMPANIONS

If you accept the idea that everything in your life is something you have chosen or asked for in some way, then be aware that this includes one of the most influential aspects of your life, i.e. the people you share it with. Life is sometimes a challenging, un-predictable and complex adventure, with many unexpected twists and turns. Each and every one of us is making our own journey and living our own life adventure: no one else can walk our path for us, regardless of how much we might wish them to, but what they can do is accompany us through life as companions, guides, allies and friends, making the journey more fun, exciting, full and fulfilling. Therefore, people whisperers are skilful at attracting and choosing good companions to accompany them on life's journey, knowing the value of being with people who bring positive qualities to the experience of life and so lovingly nurturing those relationships.

Our ability to select the right people as our companions for the journey has a huge effect on the quality and experience of everything that we do. The right companions can make the good times ecstatic and the tough times manageable.

Ask yourself:

◆ As you make your way through life, who would you like to have to accompany you?
◆ What kind of qualities will the people need to have to best help and support you, to live your most loving, successful and ultimately fulfilling life?

With six billion people out there in the world, choosing friends and companions from amongst them can be some task! In a sense, everyone in our lives is playing a role in our live's journey. These roles are very varied: from partners, close family to work colleagues, to friends, teachers, spiritual guides, lovers, rivals – the list is endless. Fate, the Universe, chance, luck or whatever we want to call it, will bring many people into our lives, some of whom come to teach us; some to support us; some to stretch us; some bearing gifts; some to create magnificent experiences with us; some to challenge us; some to love us for who we are, and some - it may seem – to do nothing much at all. It is up to us to decide who to keep in our lives and who to pass by. Likewise, we alone can decide how to integrate the people we choose in our lives and whether we will create something worth while together with them, or whether we will choose to squander the opportunities and special gifts that different people bring to us.

Problem-solvers or Problem-makers

Wouldn't it be nice if other people could solve our problems for us? But unfortunately, no one else can sort them out for us, no matter how much we may like them to. (Although people sometimes appear to create our problems very effectively for us, don't they?) Even if the people close to us can't give us the answers, they can help us to find them. Likewise, they cannot walk the path for us, but they can smooth our passage and help us along the way.

The trouble is that sometimes we invite companions along who seem to make the path through life even harder to walk. Yet it may be that the challenge of walking with these difficult people strengthens us for our own good or that the difficult people are not making the journey more challenging – those challenging people actually *are* the journey.

Suggestion:

Think of every person who is significant in your life right now . . .

- Are they currently helping you or hindering you on your journey?
- Are they making it easier or harder for you to live your life to its full glory?
- If they are hindering you or making life harder, look for the gifts, the ways you may benefit from what they are bringing: we invite people into our lives because they all bring potential gifts for us, whether they appear to or not.

On a scale of 1 to 10 (where '1' is making life impossibly difficult, where '5' is that they are neither adding nor taking away from life, and where '10' is bringing incredible value to your life), give some of your current chosen companions a score. In what ways could you view each of them differently in order to score them more highly?

Positive qualities – Positive thoughts – Positive language

The qualities we look for in our companions will depend to some extent on our own nature and the kinds of relationships and experiences we want to create. However, there are some general qualities that may be helpful if we find them in those we meet. What if you could build a fellowship of life travellers around you who could be described as follows:

Loving	Trustworthy
Courageous	Talented
Kind	Understanding
Wise	Fun
Encouraging	Flexible
Good listeners	Willing
Helpful	Centred
Patient	Inspirational

Where would you score yourself (on a scale of 1 to 10) on the above qualities? To help attract people with these qualities into your personal fellowship, you might develop more of the qualities yourself. Remember, you are travelling your journey with these people as your companions, but you will also be travelling their journey with them as their companions. The more 'desirable' qualities you possess, the more worthwhile partnerships, associates and journeys you will be invited to join. Light attracts light, positive people attract positive experiences: be around people that attract light and attract light yourself.

Things to do:

1. Think of your life as a journey and the people in your life as a fellowship of companion travellers. See how each of the companions you have chosen brings certain gifts, benefits and learning for you on your journey.
2. Enjoy the companionship of these other souls who have joined you. Feel a sense of connection and gratitude that they are willing to be a part of your story (but hopefully not your drama!).

3. Look at the roles you play in other people's fellowships and how you accompany them on their journeys.
4. If you have a clear idea of the kind of people you want as companions and stay open to allowing the right people into your life, you will be amazed at who turns up for you. For example, they say that when the pupil is ready the teacher appears. This could equally be applied to any vacancy you have in your fellowship: when you are ready to receive a certain person, they will appear, whether they are a partner, business contact, a teacher, a valuable ally, a competitor, a great friend or a soulmate.
5. See if you can catch yourself taking it all too seriously: remember, you, your life and the people in your life may simply be acting out roles in a play. Reality could be something altogether different to how we think it is.

Planning Chance Encounters!

The people whisperer knows that there are ways to increase 'good luck' and to improve the chances of successfully bringing the right people into his or her life. To enable this to happen, the people whisperer always seems to be in the right place at the right time and is adept at recognising moments of serendipity. The sort of chance encounter we are talking about could involve a life partner, a business contact, a helpful person along the way or any manner of pieces of the jigsaw we need and possibly thought we might never find.

During the lunch break at a workshop on which I was coaching, a friend who is a brilliant head of training and development in a multinational corporation turned and asked me an amusing and seemingly paradoxical question, 'So, Perry, how do you plan chance encounters?' In essence this question sounds like a contradiction in terms. But, in reality, much of what creates luck, possibilities and success can be put down to exactly that . . . planning chance encounters!

Creating the chance encounter
Bumping into the right people will help you create the life you want to live, so here are some questions to get you thinking about how to create productive chance encounters:

◆ What social and business circles do you move in?
◆ How do you encounter the right people (by chance)? How do you know they are the right people? What do you do with them when you meet them?
◆ What invitations do you receive? What invitations do you create? What invitations do you give?
◆ What limiting beliefs do you have about your ability to meet people or to mix in different circles?
◆ Have you tried 'asking' for the person you want to appear in your life without worrying about 'how' they will come? What might happen if you let go of limitations based on what you think is possible and allow the right person to come to you?
◆ How much are you pushing and *trying*, as opposed to asking for what you want and 'allowing' it to come to you?
◆ What could you do differently in your life to open up new channels and allow new people to come in?
◆ Are you being too specific or picky about the people that you think you want?

Meeting the right people

How can we define who the 'right' people are? In a sense, we could say that everyone who comes into our life is the right person: it is what we choose to do with the opportunities presented by each person that will shape our belief about whether they are 'right' or 'wrong' for us. We can be sure that whatever and whoever is in our life at this moment is right for us at this moment. We are always free to choose again, to reach out, to move forwards or sideways in order to create more chance encounters and bring new people into our lives: it is what we make of these encounters that matters in the end.

How to nurture chance encounters

◆ Be in the right state when you meet someone; be your true self.
◆ Let go of any judgements or preconceived ideas.
◆ Be patient, give people the time and space they need without pushing.

- Be interested in other people for who they are, not for what they can do for you.
- Let them talk, ask them interested questions, give them space to bring what they want to bring to your life.
- See what you could offer to them: it needs to be a two-way exchange.
- Speak their language.
- Avoid playing games.
- Trust.
- Take your time.
- If you need to, choose a good moment to ask for what you want in clear, direct language.

Coincidences and synchronicity

Think about the following:

- Do you see life as a bunch of accidents happening to you one after another: some good, some bad and some indifferent?
- Do you think the people you meet fall into your life like the chance tumble of a dice?
- Do you think the chaos theory is chaotic?
- Do you notice how many coincidences are happening in your life?
- Have you ever met someone and then said 'What a small world'?
- Have you noticed how, once you start to recognise coincidences, they seem to keep happening more and more?

Margrit and My Story

My first book was a specialist title about horse riding. When it was first published I did various appearances and shows to promote it at equestrian venues. One day some friends of mine with a horse-business asked me to share a stand with them at a small localised 'equine fair' some distance from my home. Although I was reluctant to go, not least because I did not think that the sales on the stand would justify the cost, I agreed to do it, saying, 'Well, you never know who you might meet'.

So I went along to the two-day equine fair with those words ringing around in my head. On the last day I left our stand to take a walk around other stands. One stand was for a regional newspaper that published a regular equestrian page and so I began talking to the editor. She said that she would like to run a couple of features about me – one about my horse book and one about my work coaching executives in leadership and communication – which I thought was rather exciting.

But that was only the beginning of a day of chance encounters, because the editor then turned and introduced me to a lady standing behind her, who had a pile of books laid out on the table. This lady was Margrit Coates, who is widely known for her healing work with animals and for her books, Hands-on Healing for Pets *and* Healing for Horses, *copies of which she was signing. I spent some time talking to Margrit and we exchanged contact details and swapped books.*

As a result of that meeting with Margrit, an incredible chain of life-changing events and opportunities have unfolded and continue to unfold for me. Margrit and I formed a partnership and produced and recorded an album of healing music that became the record company's best-seller of the year. (I now continue to produce music both with Margrit and as a solo artist for the same record company: this is more significant if you appreciate that I had previously spent over ten years attempting to get a recording contract and not succeeded.) Margrit also introduced me to new clients for my corporate coaching business; but more exciting than all of that, she was instrumental in this book – Secrets of the People-Whisperer – being published. Wow! How 'lucky' was all that?

All that, and more, is happening because of one 'planned chance encounter' in an unlikely setting. I had gone to the fair with the idea that 'You never know who you might meet' and that single thought opened the way for the Universe to send someone my way who was to have a huge influence and benefit on the following years of my life and career.

The story above gives a very obvious example of planning a chance encounter. Of course, chance encounters usually happen in more subtle ways than my meeting with Margrit and they aren't normally pre-empted with a phrase such as 'You never know who you might meet', but it shows just what can happen when we hold intentions and are open to possibilities. Of course, some people would just say my meeting was down to pure luck and if that is what they want to call it, well, I guess they are right:

my question in response to that would be 'Well, what can I do to allow more of that kind of "luck" to happen?'

Things to do:

1. Go somewhere different to your usual haunts: put yourself about a bit! If your social life has a routine to it, change the routine for a week and see what happens.
2. Do something you have dreamed of doing, and not got around to so far, such as taking up evening classes, going to the gym or travelling the world. Make sure it is something that will bring you into contact with people you don't know.
3. Ask your unconscious, or the Universe, or whatever power you believe in, for what you want to happen, and then forget about it.
4. Start noticing coincidences: the more you notice them and acknowledge their happening, the more they will start to work for you.
5. Always be your true self; be the best, most natural person you can be.

Soul Connection

On one level, we are all ONE. We are all connected. There is no separation. This can be a challenging idea to accept, because society and everyone within it acts with such self-interest that the idea of separation has become normal to us. But 'separation' is actually a concept that develops in us as we grow up from babyhood: as babies we are not aware of any separation; we experience ourselves as a part of the same whole as our environment and everyone in it.

As adults, we remain connected on a physical level; we just don't have a constant awareness of it. For example, if a giant meteorite hit the earth, who would die? Probably all of us! We are all connected by our existence on the same planet: we share the same home, circulate the same resources such as water and breathe the same air as one another. When a nuclear accident happens thousands of miles away, we too are affected. Even our genes go back to the same few sources. We are all part of this vast creation; we are all part of humankind: behind all the behaviour, we are all one.

◆ If you always had a sense that we are all part of the same 'One-ness', how might that alter your dealings with each and every person in your life?

People whisperers are aware that we are all connected and are all part of one creation; they are constantly in touch with that sense of connection and therefore approach all people with understanding and empathy, seeing themselves in each and every other person on the planet.

Dissolving the Gap

To fully experience the reality of our soul connection, we have to know ourselves as the other person and the other person as ourselves. Mmm! This is not necessarily as intimate as it sounds. What it means is that we sense that there is no gap or space between us and any other person, whereas normally we feel that there is an 'us', and then over there is 'them'. One definition of love means identifying others as part of ourselves, and ourselves as part of them. Imagine looking at a sunset: instead of 'you' looking at the sunset, you become a part of the moment, part of the picture of the sunset. Rather than just being the onlooker, you are in the picture and an integral part of the scene.

Being able to experience the 'connection' between us has huge potential when it comes to our encounters with other people. If we can sense the connection without experiencing a gap between ourselves and others, we will find it easier to drop judgement, to understand the other person more deeply, and to feel full compassion and empathy for them. Experiencing the connection means that we won't be inclined to erect barriers or create difficulties that hinder our interaction with the other people and results in others being inexplicably drawn towards us. By holding the space and bridging the gap or divide between us, in a sense we actually *become* love. The word 'love' carries with it all sorts of interpretations and connotations, but what we are talking about here is not love that makes us romantic, fluffy or nicey-nice. The kind of love we are talking about is beyond all of the human expressions such as words (which is why I'm struggling here!). It is powerful and is a supreme state of awareness: in it, we are totally open but also safe.

This level of soul connection can exist between you and anyone, should you choose to recognise it. Sometimes words are not enough: those are the times when we need to communicate on a soul level. If we are in a conversation and find we share no common ground whatsoever with the person to whom we are talking, we can still connect with them on this soul level by consciously dissolving the gap between us. As you can imagine, this opens up huge possibilities in areas where conversation is difficult, in all kinds of situations and relationships. We can all do this – you can do it, anyone can do it. However, be aware that attempting to use a soul connection to influence someone else intentionally for our own gain does not really work: the universal law of love will not enable us to control others in this way.

Recognising Soulmates

It is a strange phenomenon that out of the vast number of people with whom we have contact throughout our lives, there are usually a few with whom we experience a special connection – sometimes even on first meeting them. In truth we have a soul connection with everybody, but it is easier for us to recognise ourselves mirrored in some people than it is with others.

For example, have you ever met someone and hit it off with that person straight away: you feel like you already know that person – you have so much to say and seem to have so much in common? What is that about? Sometimes, even before we really talk to someone new there may be a sense of 'recognition' between us: they seem familiar, even though we know we haven't met them before. Some people explain this experience by saying it is about knowing each other before in past lives. Well, I can't honestly remember living before so I can't comment about reincarnation etc., but whatever is actually happening, encountering a soulmate is a profound experience.

Why do these soulmates come into our lives? As the sense of recognition is very real, let's accept that the reasons for their coming to us are also significant and very real. Without contriving reasons or purposes for their coming, we can enjoy the opportunity to spend time with people who come into our lives in significant ways. By allowing things to unfold gradually between us, we will discover what gifts we have for them and what gifts or messages they have for us.

Distance communication

Have you ever noticed how it is sometimes possible to communicate – without using the phone or the internet – with people despite there being a huge distance between you? Many of us in modern society find it difficult to believe in this level of communication: after all, how could we possibly hear someone communicating with us over huge distances? You don't believe it either? What about radio: do you believe in that?

There are many records of animals and people, often belonging to older tribes such as those of the African bushmen, who appear to be able to communicate over great distances with those with whom they have close relationships. As with so many of our innate skills and instincts, in the Western world we have lost touch to a large degree with these parts of ourselves. We can liken losing these skills to the way that a muscle will waste and the neural pathways to that muscle go to sleep when they are not used for any extended period. As with a muscle or neural pathway, it is not impossible to reawaken these skills, but it does require regular use and practise. A quote from the *I Ching*, a Chinese oracle from three thousand years ago says:

> Whenever a feeling is voiced with truth and frankness, whenever a deed is the clear expression of sentiment, a mysterious and far-reaching influence is exerted. At first it acts on those who are inwardly receptive. But the circle grows larger and larger. The root of all influence lies in one's own inner being: given true and vigorous expression in word and deed, its effect is great.

With openness and a soul connection, we may find that we are communicating with someone not necessarily in words, but with an aligned sense of being. We may often discover after the event that someone with whom we have a soul connection was talking about the same unlikely subject as we were on the same day. Or we go to pick up the phone to call someone but the phone rings and it is the person we were going to call who has called us instead. Although we are almost totally unaware on a mental level, which is where most of our attention in life is placed, there can be much communication happening on a soul level, and since distance is irrelevant at the soul level, this can happen with someone anywhere else in the world.

If you haven't really noticed this before, that doesn't mean it's not happening in your own life. Have you noticed how, when you buy a new car, you suddenly see so many of the same type of car on the road as yours? Previously you may not have really *seen* them: suddenly they are everywhere! (Unless you just bought yourself an Aston Martin, I suppose.)

Things to do:

1. Become aware of the fabulous gift of connection you have with certain people on a soul level. See these people as huge blessings in your life.

2. Let yourself be open to the idea that you are connected to absolutely everyone. Actually you could take it beyond all the people you see and feel that connection with the whole of your surroundings. Just because other people don't recognise the same level of connection as you, or just because they even 'act' obnoxiously towards you doesn't mean you are not connected on a deeper level. Sometimes people may even act obnoxiously towards you because your soul connection with them makes it 'safe' for them to do so.

3. Start to notice when people at a distance from you appear to be thinking along the same lines.

Conclusion

The ways of exploring people whispering are infinite. In working our way through the twelve secrets, we have looked at everything from awareness of our own physical, mental and spiritual communication through to how we interact with the Universe and others at soul level. Here are a few more isolated thoughts – golden nuggets – for you to reflect and expand upon:

◆ Keep communication clear and simple.
◆ *Try* less and allow life to flow.
◆ Be aware of the fear of being vulnerable: remember that a newborn baby is about as vulnerable as a human can possibly be, but it still gets taken care of.
◆ Timing is so important: if you time your communication with someone just right, their response will be much more favourable than if your timing was inappropriate. You have to develop patience and sensitivity to how people feel and where they are 'at', in order to have great timing.
◆ Flexibility is a key skill to have around people. Life is in a constant state of flux; nothing stays the same, including people. To be the best you can be and allow others to be the best they can be, don't assume that doing what worked before will work the same next time: it may not. Move with the flow and be flexible at all times. Doing A may result in B on one occasion: that does not mean that doing A next time will result in B, it may result in X!
◆ Gossip . . . does not do anyone any favours!
◆ Age: ask any adult and I think you will find that most people, especially the elderly, feel about seventeen to twenty-one years old. That is an interesting thing to bear in mind when talking to someone of seventy-five!

- This is your life: it is not about anyone else or what they would do. Listen to people's opinions, by all means, but at the end of the day, choose what you feel and know to be right for you.
- Keep moving forwards. If you try to go backwards in life or ponder too long on what happened before, such as how someone hurt you or let you down, you will miss what is happening now.
- Be encouraging: to yourself and anyone else that is around. Encouragement brings a positive boost of energy to people.
- Laugh more than you would normally!
- Remember that life is short: if possible, make your peace with the people around you, without compromising yourself in the process.
- In any situation where you are 'stuck' or don't know what to do, come up with at least three options and then choose one. You may be in a situation with someone where you don't think you have any options, and externally that may be true, but you always have options about how you communicate with yourself or how you feel.

So, who is the people whisperer? In reality, we all have a people whisperer inside us: an adept, sensitive and skilful communicator who is often hidden behind a mask of conditioning and automatic responses born out of fear, social expectations and limiting beliefs, or buried under the weight of coping with everyday life. The wonderful thing is that when we begin to remove all that is *not* us, we can begin to allow the inner people whisperer within us to surface and communicate with ourselves, with other people and with our environment on a new-found level of joy, engagement and success.

As we practise the methods of people whispering and integrate them more and more into our communication, relationships and our life, we will begin to discover another secret: that opening ourselves to the art of people whispering – the skill of communicating with ourselves, others and the Universe – is an ever-expanding process. There are endless possibilities to be uncovered along the way.

May you discover the people whisperer within you and may the art of communication enhance your own life and the lives of all those beings with whom you share your world.

Resources

For further information about
Secrets of The People Whisperer
seminars and workshops worldwide,
visit: www.thepeoplewhisperer.com